HANDMADE RUGS

WILLIAM HENRY HARRISON ON HORSEBACK AND THE FAMOUS LOG CABIN, A CAMPAIGN EMBLEM, APPEAR IN NEEDLE-
WORK IN THE CENTRE OF THIS RUG; THE BORDER IS OF WOOLEN CLOTH, CUT IN STRIPS, FULLED ON A THREAD,
THEN SEWED IN PLACE. THE "HARRISON MAT," NOW OWNED BY MRS. ELIZABETH H. RUSSELL, WAS
MADE ABOUT 1840, BY MARY VINTON, OF EAST BRAINTREE, MASSACHUSETTS

HANDMADE RUGS

By

ELLA SHANNON BOWLES

With Many Illustrations
Some of Them in Color

GARDEN CITY PUBLISHING COMPANY, INC.

Garden City   New York

1937

GARDEN CITY PUBLISHING COMPANY, INC.

PRINTED IN THE UNITED STATES OF AMERICA

To the memory of my mother
Myra E. Berry Shannon

FOREWORD

My interest in handmade rugs began years ago, as I watched my grandmother create hooked and braided rugs for the yellow-painted floors of her weather-stained New Hampshire farmhouse.

This interest in rugs, especially the variety known as hooked, pulled, or drawn-in, was revived when I came to live in a community where many of the women spent hours of the long winters in making them. Mr. and Mrs. Robert P. Peckett, of Sugar Hill, New Hampshire, first pointed out to me the possibilities of the revival of this old New England handicraft. Through their courtesy and coöperation I published in the *Modern Priscilla* my first article on the subject, "Rug-Making in the New Hampshire Hills." The contents of this little volume are the result of study and investigation for the preparation of material on rug-making which has been since published in various magazines. If much of the material in the book is drawn from New England, this is not because I am unaware that the handiwork which I have described is made in various other sections of the country, but simply because I am familiar with the work as it is done here.

E. S. B.

ACKNOWLEDGMENTS

I wish to thank the editors of the *Antiquarian*, the *Dearborn Independent*, the *Modern Priscilla*, the *Woman's World*, *Forecast*, *Holland's*, *Illustrated Needlework*, the *Christian Science Monitor*, and *Art in Australia* for allowing me to republish articles and pictures which have appeared in their periodicals during the past years.

I am also most grateful to the director of the South End House Industry, Boston, to the Massachusetts Normal Art School, to Mrs. Mary Meigs Atwater of the Shuttle Craft Weavers, to Mrs. Parker W. Whittemore, Mrs. Mary Perkins Taylor, and to the editors of the *House Beautiful*, the *Modern Priscilla*, *Antiques*, and the *Country Gentleman* for permission to make use of their photographs. The rugs which have been reproduced in color were generously lent by Mrs. Elizabeth H. Russell, Mrs. J. F. Sheppard, James M. Shoemaker Co., Inc., New York, and the South End House Industry, Boston.

To make a book of this type of value other sources than the study of rugs made by the author must be consulted. I extend my appreciation, therefore, to the editors of the *Antiquarian*, of *Antiques*, and of the *Modern Priscilla* for allowing me to quote directly from their magazines; to Mr. Ralph W. Burnham for granting me permission to cite illustrations from his booklets on hooked rugs, and to the President of the North American Dye Corporation for permission to quote from *Modern Home Dyeing*.

I have received inspiration from the booklet, *Abnakee Rugs*, written by Miss Helen R. Albee, and personal assistance from Mr. Robert P. Peckett, Miss Sybil Nash, Mrs. Ernest Poole, Miss L. A. Phillips, and Mrs. Gertrude DeWager. To all of these, to those who kindly allowed me the use of their rugs for study and for photographs, and to the women of the New Hampshire hills who coöperated in the gathering of the old-time dye recipes, I offer my sincere thanks.

E. S. B.

CONTENTS

ILLUSTRATIONS

ILLUSTRATIONS

HANDMADE RUGS

HANDMADE RUGS

I

NOTES ON THE HISTORY OF HOOKED RUGS

THE strains of the wedding march pealed through the house. Preceding the bride were her maids, lovely in their gowns of sweet-pea hues. Then, on the arm of her father, the bride came down the long room to meet the groom, who was waiting under the floral arch. All was most conventional, most correct — a fashionable home wedding.

The wedding guest beside me touched my arm.

"Do you see upon what Priscilla and Roger are to stand while the ceremony is being performed?" she whispered. "It's his present to her, I understand."

Certainly it was a most unusual bridal gift — a large drawn-in rug, bearing a wreath of old-time posies worked out upon a background of softest tan, all the colors mellowed and beautified by the passing of time!

The bride was famed for her love of the traditions of bygone days, and it was rumored that the newly wedded pair was to leave for the honeymoon on horseback in ancient Colonial fashion. Knowing her tastes, friends had sent gifts of pewter, reproductions of early cottage furniture, and glistening Sandwich glass. But Priscilla counted the hooked rug, made years before by a forgotten craftswoman in a New

England farmhouse, as one of her most cherished possessions, and planned that it should occupy a place of honor in her country home — not on the floor, but on the wall of the entrance hall.

Let me describe this rug, for you might like to copy it. It was rectangular in shape, about three feet wide and five feet long. The foundation was of fine burlap; the loops were pulled through to an eighth of an inch in height and were left unclipped. The background was a soft café-au-lait in color, and I am sure that all-wool material was used in the process of hooking in, because all of the loops had lost color alike by the passing of time. The floral design was simple — a wreath of soft-toned pink roses and leaves in the centre, and corner patterns of the same flowers. As I told you, the rug was large, but it was so finely made that it could be readily pulled through a small hoop.

Such rugs as this have been made for many years by the country and village women of New England, Nova Scotia, Newfoundland, the Provinces, New York, Pennsylvania, and some parts of the South. I have also heard of prized family hooked rugs crossing the continent in the days of the "Covered Wagon." A woman living in California recently wrote me that she owned a rug carried by her grandmother from Maine early in the fifties.

The earliest history of the making of hooked rugs is wrapped in mystery. To quote the editor of

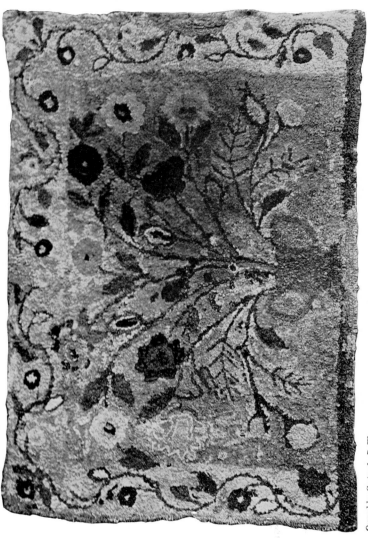

THIS RUG WAS MADE BY THE OWNER'S GRANDMOTHER, AND MRS. DeWAGER BELIEVES IT TO BE ONE OF THE FIRST HOOKED RUGS EVER MADE. THE DESIGN IS A COLONIAL PORCH WITH FLOWER-ENTWINED PILLARS. THE VASE RESTING ON THE FLOOR OF THE PORCH CONTAINS SUNFLOWERS OF ATTAR COLOR, RED AND WHITE ROSES AND BUDS, A CALLA LILY AND LEAF, FERN FRONDS, AND A FEW INDIGO-BLUE FLOWERS

Antiques, in a note appended to an article, "A Memory of Grandmother's Mats," by Gertrude DeWager, published in June 1925: "The history of hooked rugs is buried so deeply beneath unsubstantial tradition and romantic legend as almost to defy efforts to unearth reliable fragments of it."

This statement is borne out by other authorities. The secretary of the Essex Institute at Salem, Massachusetts, wrote me that he had no information as to date in regard to hooked rugs. The librarian of the New Hampshire Historical Society wrote, "Unfortunately we are unable to date any of our hooked rugs." The curator of the Memorial Hall at Deerfield, Massachusetts, answered my question in regard to her knowledge of the age of hooked rugs by saying: "Different kinds of rugs were made in the nineties and probably earlier. At that time they were sold and brought a considerable income to the makers. My mother had hooked rugs made by a relative in Vermont — I think in the seventies."

But there are authorities who claim that the hooked rug has great age. Let me quote from one of the booklets written by Mr. Ralph W. Burnham of Ipswich, Massachusetts: — "Several prominent writers upon the subject strongly contend that the deservedly popular floor covering antedates the American Revolution. A still more venturesome writer of reputation asserts that hooked rugs were in evidence earlier than the year 1700."

In an article, "Hooked Rugs," published in the *Antiquarian* in May 1925, Mary Johnson Carey tells us that "it was among the first floor coverings to grace an American hearthstone, and the date of its advent may be placed in the early part of the eighteenth century."

It is pleasant to believe this, even if we cannot prove it, and I see no reason to doubt that women who knew the arts of making samplers, embroidering coats of arms upon cherished bits of satin, and working "mourning pieces," did hooked-in or drawn-in pictures upon loosely woven linens, to be used as floor coverings in their "best rooms." The early nineteenth century at least produced home-knitted mittens, which were decorated with hooked-in patterns of gay wools.

I like to think that it was the desire for creative expression, as well as the proverbial Yankee thrift, that inspired the handicraft workers of bygone days in their making of rugs. When sleety rains beat against the windowpanes of low-eaved farmhouses, or drifting snows shut out the rest of the world, what more fascinating occupation than planning designs, coloring fabrics with vegetable dyes made at home from barks and herbs, and then lovingly working out the patterns with bits of wool! Some of the rugs were poorly made and crude in coloring, but others were works of art and expressed the simple individuality of a peaceful and contented people.

I am of the opinion that any rug, if the design was original, was a form of art. Professor Mason says: "The first woman making a change in any natural object for the gratification which it afforded her is the starting point of three evolutions: that of art itself, whether textile, plastic, or musical; of herself, in the practice of it, growing out of a mere imitator to be a creator; of the universal or public appreciation of art, or what might be called racial or tribal imagination."

Katharine Lee Bates tells us in her *American Literature* that "a dozen factories were gathered into the farmhouse kitchen, where thin-lipped women baked and brewed, washed and ironed, canned and pickled, compounded the family physic of 'snail-water,' with ruby jellies to obliterate its taste, spun, wove, knit, quilted, made candles, soap, sausages, rag carpets, feather beds, and were by turns seamstresses, milliners, tailors, with frequent calls away to dairy, poultry yard, and milking stool."

So it lightens the picture a little, I think, to believe that women of old New England responded to the creative urge, and designed and executed works of art in the form of hooked rugs for use in their own homes and for their daughters' "setting-out."

There is one test which you may safely apply to hooked rugs when you are trying to tell a little about their age, and that is the kind of material used to make the foundation. We are told that cotton cloth was not made in England until after the year 1760, so it seems probable that it was not in common use in America until the beginning of the nineteenth century. It would be safe to say that a rug hooked in on homespun and home-woven linen was probably made during the period when such materials were manufactured. But there is one point against the statement — the thrift of New England women. I once found a rug made on old-time cloth, while evidence proved that the rug was not very old, for the economical worker had used for her foundation some home-woven cloth found in the house. Burlaps, too, varied in kind; and after a little experience you can tell the older type from that more recently made.

I have discovered no record of hooked rugs in old wills; but in the inventory of the estate of Nathaniel Shannon, who died in Portsmouth, New Hampshire, in the latter part of the eighteenth century, I find listed, together with a Negro man named Prince, valued at four hundred pounds, a woman and child, — woman called Diana, — valued at three hundred pounds, one half dozen "turkey work'd chairs," and among the other household furnishings, two rugs valued at twelve pounds and ten shillings. There is absolutely no proof that these rugs were of the hooked variety, but the mentioning of them in the inventory is interesting to the collector.

Hooked rugs were made by the German women of early Pennsylvania, and examples of their work are

THE SIMPLE DESIGN USED ON THIS ANTIQUE HOOKED RUG IS AN EXPRESSION OF THE CREATIVE INSTINCT OF SOME BEAUTY-LOVING WOMAN

still in existence. An especially interesting photograph of one of their quaint products is shown in the *Practical Book of Early American Arts and Crafts*, by Eberlein and McClure. In describing it, the authors say: — "At other times the worker was not so conservative and modest in her aims, but, like the Pennsylvania Dutch woman who wrought the little rug in the plate illustration, embarked on an ambitious scheme beyond her powers of proper execution, and achieved a result janglingly garish in juxtaposition of magentas, scarlets, and emerald greens, and startlingly grotesque in design. Such pieces of handiwork may be interesting and quaint, but cannot be esteemed for beauty."

In New England, hooked rugs reached the height of their popularity in the Civil War period. It is unfortunate that many of the products of the years following the war were crude in design and coloring, for the commercial rug-patterns of the time were hideous.

If you are interested in using your imagination to trace by their designs the development of the making of hooked rugs, you have plenty of material at your disposal. The earliest rugs show delicate vine borders and realistic baskets and sprays of flowers, drawn upon the background without attention to formal design. Black outlines were seldom used, and the coloring was usually soft and pleasing. Mary Johnson Carey suggests that these soft shades can be traced to the fine embroideries and brocaded stuffs used in dress materials brought from France and England. The sampler, too, played its part in suggesting ideas for ear'y rugs. Precise and formal trees, set baskets of flowers, houses, and sometimes figures of people were introduced into rug designs, and early presidential campaigns led to the use of the patriotic symbols sometimes seen in hooked rugs of an early date.

French glassmaking influenced the designs used on articles made by the New England and Sandwich Glass Companies. In the same manner Aubusson carpet designs were copied by New England rugmakers. The woman who had ceased to think that the vines and scroll designs which her mother copied from the needlework on her petticoat were beautiful turned to the new "boughten" carpets for her patterns.

Occasionally an ambitious worker attempted the construction of an entire carpet for her parlor. I have seen the remains of one that was unusually beautiful. Evidently it was taken up when commercial carpeting came into existence, and now the small piece which remains has been made into a rug. The carpet was made of squares of black lightweight broadcloth, such as was used for "go-to-meeting" suits for men during the period preceding the Civil War. The blocks were about twelve inches square, and at the centre of each was pulled in the design of a rose with leaves surrounding it. The squares were set together with strips of canvas, filled in, "hit-or-miss," and a border of the hooked-in hit-or-miss framed the whole.

From the State of Maine came another unusual rug. It was about sixty years old and beautifully made. The design was inspired, I am sure, by one from an Aubusson carpet, but the outstanding feature was the fact that the work upon the rug was pulled in through fine unbleached cotton cloth.

A few years ago hooked rugs had little value except to their makers, who prized them as coverings for the yellow-painted floors of their forerooms and kitchens.

"I gave my son's wife a hooked rug and she used it in front of the kitchen stove," an old woman told me. "It was lots of work to make it. I thought she might have put it in her bedroom!" This shows how little hooked rugs were prized in remote rural districts until collectors and interior decorators began to seek them for use with early American furniture.

A gentleman who spent some years in Newfoundland told me that in the spring of the year wives of the fishermen put "mats," as they called them, into the frames. This man really did some constructive work by directing the women in the use of less brilliant colors and in drawing more pleasing designs for them. At that time the workers in the locality made these mats or rugs simply for their own homes, and they envied a certain worker who received the price of ten dollars for one which she had produced.

The craft of making hooked rugs is not forgotten. New England women learned the art from their mothers and grandmothers. May they teach it to their daughters!

II

COLORS FADED AND FRESH

THE Poet stood in the unkempt dooryard of the desolate house where the auction was in progress. He was clinging fondly to a couple of garishly colored hooked rugs, which were carefully draped over his angular right arm.

A stranger might have wondered at his interest in the crude products, but I understood. For I too knew the story of the drab woman who made them. In a life of tragedy so vivid that it would not ring true if written, these rugs stood for the only bits of joy and color that the maker knew. Denied by an eccentric, crabbed husband the delight of "fixing-up" the house, she hid in the corn chamber her rug frames and odds and ends of cloth which she had surreptitiously dyed. Then, when her puritanical spouse went to town, she feverishly worked to create her vision. And up there in the corn chamber, after her death, were found the rugs — crude expressions of a beauty-starved life!

But manufacturing hooked rugs was more than the urge of New England women's creative instincts, for the craft provided entertainment and occupation for the long, lonely hours of primitive country life.

The New England hooked rugs varied in shape. The most common shape seen was rectangular. Square rugs were sometimes made. Occasionally a worker produced a round or an oval rug, and octagonal or hexagonal rugs were frequently seen. One of the most unusual rugs that I have ever known was shaped like an octagon. It was a genuine antique, with a charming floral design in soft colorings, and was finished with a homemade fringe of black yarn. Perhaps the most uncommon of all was the type having an edge formed by scrolls after the fashion of centrepieces finished with buttonhole-stitch embroidery.

I was surprised to have someone ask me how these rugs of odd shape were made. The answer is simple. The desired shape was drawn on a rectangular piece of burlap, and after the hooking was completed and the work was removed from the frames the rug was cut out and completed in the manner of finishing all hooked rugs — a method which I shall describe later. Of course a rug with a scalloped edge required great care in finishing, but the method used was the same as that employed in completing the bottom of the scalloped dresses popular a few seasons ago.

Half-rugs or door rugs were made in great quantities during the seventies. As the name signifies, they were half-ovals in shape and were used before doors. Sometimes they were decorated only with simple floral or animal designs, but frequently the worker was more ambitious and added the word WELCOME, the phrase GOOD LUCK, or CALL AGAIN; or, if she had a religious turn of mind, she occasionally pulled in the sentences, GOD IS LOVE or JESUS DWELLS HERE.

Readers who love Rebecca, the whimsical child heroine created by Kate Douglas Wiggin, will recall the rug described in *More Chronicles of Rebecca:* —

"Rebecca could see the Cames' brown farmhouse from Mrs. Baxter's sitting-room window. The little-traveled road with strips of tufted green between the wheel tracks curled dustily up to the very doorstep,

Owned by Miss Sybil Nash

"WELCOME" RUGS GREETED THE GUEST AT THE DOORS OF
NEW ENGLAND FARMHOUSES

and inside the screen door of pink mosquito netting was a wonderful drawn-in rug, shaped like a half pie, with 'Welcome' in saffron letters on a green ground."

Hooked rugs varied in size. I have described one carpet, although hooked carpets were rare. One well-known collector has told me of a church carpet in Nova Scotia which was hooked in by the women of the congregation; and in an antique shop in Vermont

I saw a hooked hit-or-miss rug large enough completely to cover the floor of a small room. Hall runners, usually ornamented with conventional patterns, were sometimes made by women of the mid-Victorian period, and modern workers have copied the idea for country homes. A most unusual and interesting stair runner, bearing hooked designs of birds and animals, is in the summer home of Mrs. Parker Whittemore at West Gloucester, Massachusetts.

I have seen rugs nearly large enough to cover the floors of small rooms. Let me describe two. One made during the Civil War had a black background and a floral pattern of roses and leaves. The rug almost covered the kitchen floor of the house where I found it. Yes — kitchen, but such an immaculate New Hampshire kitchen, into which a bit of dust or scrap of lint dared not venture! The other rug was larger, but not so old; its colors were lighter, and one interesting feature was the rare shade of mauve used in the background border. This rug now occupies a place of honor in the country home of a well-known American novelist.

But not all early New England rugs were large. One of the prettiest small antique rugs that I have found was about eighteen inches long and carried a pattern of the blossoms of the snowball bush upon a light brown background.

Modern designers are making rugs in all sizes to meet every need. One expert is putting upon the

Courtesy of Mrs. Whittemore and "The House Beautiful"

A MOST UNUSUAL AND INTERESTING STAIR RUNNER, BEARING HOOKED DESIGNS OF BIRDS AND
ANIMALS, IS IN THE SUMMER HOME OF MRS. PARKER WHITTEMORE AT
WEST GLOUCESTER, MASSACHUSETTS

market a very small rug-pattern, especially for novices in the work. By starting with a small rug, the worker does not become discouraged while the hooking-in process is new to her. Large rugs like those which I have described would take many hours of tedious labor, and should be attempted only by an experienced worker.

The question of color in hooked-rug making is most important. Lovely shades have been produced in old-time rugs, especially those created during the Victorian period, when gaudy colors were in fashion, by the fading of the dyes originally used. The rug-maker of the present day may find it difficult to keep her own coloring soft and mellow, yet a rug loses its characteristic beauty if bright colors are pulled in.

In speaking of color, Helen Albee, the creator of the Abnakee rugs, says: —

"A careful study of the effects of colors upon each other will show that colors which are in themselves beautiful are often inharmonious when combined. Also, a little of a color may be good, when a larger proportion seems to destroy the balance of harmony. Success in this matter is largely a matter of close observation and experience, although some persons have a natural feeling or instinct regarding color, which is seldom in error."

Would you have the will power, after spending days in making a drawn-in rug, to hang it up in a

window where the sun shone brightly for hours, or
to lay it out on the tin roof in rain and sunshine?
But that's exactly the method of one woman who
manufactures lovely rugs. I can't tell you whether
or not the results would be always perfectly satisfactory, but I do know that this particular worker
achieves a soft blending of colors that makes her rugs
resemble family heirlooms. However, if you use subdued shades, or dye and experiment until you get
just the hues that you need, there is no reason why
your own rugs should not be things of exquisite
beauty.

Excellent ideas for color combinations are given
by the Textile Color Card Association and have been
published in a booklet on *Modern Home Dyeing*,
written by Martha Jane Phillips. The chart offers
many suggestions to the rug-maker who has not been
trained in color.

COLOR BACKGROUND	HARMONIOUS COMBINATIONS
Navy blue	Saxe blue, old gold, orange, carmine
Negro brown	Buff, peacock blue, purple, topaz
Pearl gray	Peacock blue, jade green, turquoise blue, old blue
Purple	Burnt orange, honey, old gold, castor, Negro brown, yellow
Reseda green	Chamois, purple
Salmon	Pearl gray, mode, steel
Taupe	Bright blue, amethyst, burnt orange, castor, laurel pink

OF THIS RUG ALICE VAN LEER CARRICK SAID, "IT IS THE FINEST IN COLOR AND LUSTROUS SHEEN THAT I HAVE EVER SEEN." IT WAS "PICKED UP" IN A COTTAGE IN THE CENTRAL PART OF NEW HAMPSHIRE AND IS OWNED BY MRS. FRANCES SHEPPARD OF DOVER, NEW HAMPSHIRE

Orange	Gold, blue, violet, brown, yellow
Blue-green	Purple
Red	Blue, dark green, gold
American Beauty	Fawn
Amethyst	Delft blue, gold, orchid, turquoise
Apricot	Beaver
Beige	Peacock blue
Bottle green	Apricot, topaz
Brown	Golden brown, tan, electric blue, burnt orange
Buff	Orange, Burgundy, Copenhagen, Negro brown
Burnt orange	Mahogany, peacock blue, taupe, purple
Copenhagen blue	Buff
Chestnut brown	Beaver, fawn, champagne, turquoise, apricot
Delft blue	Amethyst, gold
Ecru	Seal brown
Heliotrope	Beige
Laurel	Gray
Mahogany	Peacock, pearl gray, terra cotta, burnt orange

A. H. Church says: "Let it be remembered, however, that no rigid rules of cast iron should be allowed to trammel the imagination of the artist, to whom there are many things more important than rules, such as observation, knowledge, and experiment; a cultivated taste, sound judgment, and light fancy; an appreciation of what is meant by balance, distribution, and reticence of tone."

So, for the reasons expressed in the quotation, I

will not presume to plan color schemes for the individual worker. I will, however, offer some suggestions which have been helpful to other crafts-women.

Ivory, cream, tan, fawn, soft browns, and black are excellent colors for backgrounds. A tan centre, combined with old rose, sage green, bronze green, cream, pale yellow, and wood brown is lovely. Old rose, warm golden brown, and olive combine effectively. Reds, vivid greens, and yellows should be used sparingly; but a judicious blending of rich soft browns, rusty yellows, dull rose, deep mauve, ivory, velvety black, deep blues, gray-blue, and dull green will take any rug out of the realm of the common-place. Bits of black used to outline certain portions of the design add character to the rug.

Helen Albee suggests that, if a dull rich color predominates, rich dark colors should be used through the whole scheme; but that, if the body color is of a light tone, soft light tones of other colors are most pleasing. In her booklet on the Abnakee rugs she tells of combinations of old rose, warm golden browns, and olive; of a light Gobelin blue worked with ivory, old pink, and a light dull olive, with outlines either of dark yellow-brown or very dark bronze-green; of an ivory centre with an old-pink border worked in green; of a tan centre combined with old rose, sage green, bronze green, light yellow, cream, and dark brown outlines.

"Look around you," an artist once said to me, "and notice how Nature uses her colors."

As I have said before, these ideas are merely suggestions. If you have the rudiments of the qualities which make an artist or a creator, you will desire to plan your own color scheme and give expression to your own individuality as you experiment with "yellow, the color of gold and fire, symbolizing reason; green, the color of vegetable life, symbolizing utility and labor; red, the color of blood, symbolizing war and love; and blue, the color of the sky, symbolizing spiritual life, duty, and religion."

III

DESIGNS FOR HOOKED RUGS

"NOTHING made by man's hand can be indifferent; it must be either beautiful and elevating or ugly and degrading," said William Morris. This statement may be applied as well to hooked rugs as to any other forms of handicraft. Designs on antique hooked rugs are as varied as the personalities of the women who created them. Some were ornate; some were crude; others were beautiful and well balanced.

Historical, landscape, and picture rug-designs are most interesting to the collector. The landscape rugs are quaint and the designs are varied. A bit of fence and woodland, a house and trees like those seen on old samplers, a path leading into the woods, a ship at sea, the village green, a field with mountains beyond, are a few subjects used. Mary Johnson Carey refers to a brick-house design, which she describes as showing a "prim Colonial house occupying the centre of a rectangle. From the chimneys of the house curly puffs of smoke issue, and on either side are stiff trees and a picket fence." One designer of modern rugs, Mr. Ralph Burnham, has developed the idea of these old picture rugs and added to his patterns stage coaches and taverns, fireside scenes, and even a hunting picture.

Environment influenced designers in their choice of subjects. The rugs made by the women of the

Cranberry Islands, Maine, were typical of seafaring life, their designs being suggested by lines left on the sand by the tide, by waves lapping on the beach, by seaweeds, and shells, and the tips of distant sails seen at sea.

I am indebted to Mary Johnson Carey for this information from her article on hooked rugs published in the *Antiquarian* for May 1925: "The whaling industry, which centred in New Bedford, Nantucket, and Long Island, claiming nearly all able-bodied men in the New England seaport towns, has been picturesquely commemorated in the hooked rugs. Made by the women during the long months of their men's absence, their destiny was often the cabin of some whaling ship. A full-rigged schooner usually formed the central part of the design, and appropriate nautical objects, such as anchors, cables, etc., appear in the border."

Rugs perfected by workers in Labrador, under the patronage of Dr. Grenfell, show how the modern hooked rug is influenced by environment for its patterns. Not long ago I saw one, used in the nursery of a country home in the White Mountains, showing the picture of a dog team — the sledge, the snow, and evergreen trees.

Did you know that the laying of the Atlantic telegraph cable influenced the patterns used in American handicrafts? The cable pattern is frequently seen on pieces of Sandwich glass, and it is sometimes found on hooked rugs. Mr. Robert P. Peckett of Sugar Hill, New Hampshire, owns a rare rug bearing an exquisite floral pattern framed with an endless-chain border, which surely must have developed from the Atlantic-cable idea.

The hit-or-miss rug was made, I am sure, to use up odds and ends of left-over materials. As the name implies, the centres were variegated, but the borders were usually of solid black. I have seen one hit-or-miss rug with a star in the centre and the remainder of the work done with many different colors.

Conventional patterns were the simplest designs used by the old-time rug-makers. I have found hooked rugs marked off with a brick; patterns made by drawing around dessert plates and "butter chips"; designs carried out in diamonds, squares, and ovals. One very uncommon pattern was made by a woman in a New Hampshire village. She told me that she dropped a spot of ink upon a paper and, folding the paper, cut out the motif formed. This she arranged upon her background, gaining an Oriental effect. "Down East" a rainbow rug was made, and you will at once guess that it shaded in the prismatic colors of red, orange, yellow, green, blue, and violet. Shell rugs are common in Nova Scotia, and the sunshine-and-shadow design, made of small brightly colored squares upon a dark background, is also a popular pattern.

You can unearth animal rugs in any New England

Courtesy of Playderman and Kaufman, Boston

ENVIRONMENT INFLUENCED DESIGNERS IN THEIR CHOICE OF SUBJECTS, AND RUGS MADE BY THE
WOMEN OF SEAPORT TOWNS WERE TYPICAL OF SEAFARING LIFE

FLORAL RUG WITH ENDLESS-CHAIN BORDER, POSSIBLY INSPIRED BY THE LAYING OF THE ATLANTIC CABLE

village. They were made in great quantities during the middle of the nineteenth century, and chickens, ducklings, cows, kittens, and horses posed that their portraits might be preserved in worsteds. Only once was I shown a rug upon which lounged an animal whose like I had never seen before; his proud owner told me that he was a lion! Only his flowing mane bore any resemblance to the king of the jungle. He might have been almost anything from a gentle tabby cat to a wild dog. But his creator was not lacking in imagination, for she had added to the unhappy appearance of the rug by sewing yellow glass buttons in place for the beast's eyes. The workmanship was unexcelled and the rug was soft in texture, but I felt that long hours of patient labor had been wasted. So often animal patterns are not entirely satisfactory.

I have seen an adorable pattern showing a perky kitten lapping milk from a blue bowl, and many door rugs upon which sat majestic house cats. Even parrots, birds of paradise, and peacocks have invaded the realm of the hooked rug.

The floral patterns made by our great-grandmothers were the loveliest of all. They were arranged in wreaths and sprays, which were sometimes combined with corner designs and scrolls, and occasionally the horn of plenty was adapted for use in the pattern. During the period when young America was first beginning to feel her opulence, the horn of plenty was a popular design in the products of many crafts, and it is natural that it should appear on hooked rugs.

"I made lots o' horn-o'-plenty rugs when I was a young girl," said a woman who has spent nearly ninety years in the New Hampshire hills. "Would you like to know how I marked off my designs? I laid a piece of paper down on a horn-o'-plenty somebody had hooked in on a rug, and pricked over the design with a needle. Then I took a piece of burnt wood and rubbed over the holes, and my pattern would show on my foundation."

A lovely antique rug owned by Mr. Peckett has a pattern of pansies sprinkled here and there upon the background. In some of the old rugs, wreaths and bouquets of flowers were hooked higher than the background. A beautiful rug of this type, once exhibited as an almost perfect example of an old hooked rug, is owned by Mrs. Daisie Colby of Franconia, New Hampshire. This rug has the added charm of being a family heirloom.

Exquisite are the designs inspired by the posies of old New England gardens. Wreaths of roses, sprays of lilies, bluebells, heartsease, "pinies," yellow daisies, "laylocks," and hollyhocks run riot on backgrounds of soft gray, mellow tan, old ivory, and black. In these designs as in no others is the hand of the artist apparent. At an auction in Vermont I saw one of these floral rugs which filled me with the spirit of

THE HOUSE CAT SOMETIMES SERVED AS A MODEL FOR THE DESIGN OF A HOOKED RUG

THIS DESIGN SHOWS THE "KING OF BEASTS" SURROUNDED BY BEAUTIFULLY SHADED ROSES, THUS COMBINING THE ATMOSPHERE OF THE JUNGLE WITH THAT OF A NEW ENGLAND GARDEN!

covetousness. Time had subdued the original colorings, and the work was so expertly done that the flowers seemed to have been thrown down upon the background after being gathered in the garden behind the ancient house.

Here is the place, I am sure, for me to speak of the development of the modern floral pattern. Sometimes a beautiful design just happens. I know of a village woman who made a semiconventional rose pattern, happened to arrange it pleasingly, and designed a rug said by a French artist to be a true example of a fine art. All this is chance, as I have said, but there is another type of worker who is developing the artistic possibilities of the hooked rug. This is the trained designer, who is developing the handicraft as has Martha Ross Titcomb, whose rugs, with their soft, harmonious colors, meet William Morris's test of being "beautiful and elevating."

Oriental influence is seen occasionally in rug designs. Evidently some workers have deliberately copied rugs from Eastern countries. The Paisley shawl, — itself an imitation of Cashmere textiles, — may have contributed the motif of the palm figure. One writer tells of several old rugs which he found Down East. They bore the palm pattern worked in deep reds, greens, and browns with a filler of black, and were in design and workmanship quite as lovely as some of the Oriental rugs.

In the Abnakee rugs designed by Helen Albee,

simple forms are used. In speaking of design, Miss Albee says in her booklet, *Abnakee Rugs:* "I should recommend the designer to study savage ornament, semicivilized design, and Indian patterns; also bowls, basketry, and textiles made by the Zunis, the Chiriquians, the North Coast and Navajo Indians, and the Peruvians. Fine examples are to be found among the Pacific Islanders. Here are fresh and interesting forms and ideas that can be adapted — not copied — for the uses of hooked rugs."

Well-made Indian baskets will furnish ideas, and a thorough study of the decoration used on them will furnish inspiration for the rug-designer. The maker of baskets gleaned her designs from nature and its forces — from flowers, trees, lightning, ripples on the water, a flock of geese against the sky, clouds, and mountains.

One woman who sells rugs tells me that she is successful in disposing of patterns having a plain border and a simple central motif upon a background of contrasting color. Other designers are making rugs carrying out the patterns found on chintzes, or simple designs displaying the color scheme of the hangings in some room.

Blue-and-white hooked rugs are always lovely, and patterns for them are sometimes adapted from pieces of old china.

The modern commercial rug pattern is not to be spurned, however — that is, if good taste is employed

THE BACKGROUND OF THIS OLD HOOKED RUG IS GRAY. THE CENTRE DESIGN IS COPIED FROM FLOWERS
IN AN OLD-TIME GARDEN, AND IS PULLED IN HIGHER THAN THE BACKGROUND

Courtesy of the South End House Industry, Boston

QUAINT LADIES, DRINKING TEA, NOW APPEAR ON HOOKED RUGS. THIS SILHOUETTE DESIGN IS WORKED OUT IN DEEP BLUE, BUT DIFFERENT COLOR SCHEMES MAY BE USED

in its selection. Some of the modern patterns are made by true artists; others are not. It is well to get in touch with a designer who you know has given the subject much thought. Many of the popular women's magazines show patterns for hooked rugs which carry out the ideas of the old-time rugs or bring out the points of the best modern products. Still, there is a joy in creating your own patterns as your great-grandmother created hers. If your rug is expertly pulled and of good color, it may become an heirloom, and your children's children may point with pride to the exquisite design made by their grandmother. Perhaps you will be like one of the old-time workers of whom Gertrude DeWager speaks in her article, "A Memory of Grandmother's Mats": —

"And it happened now and again that some unknown genius of the hills has torn a beauty-haunted soul to shreds and pieced it together once more on coarse burlap with bright-hued fragments of discarded clothing. When she had done the work, she had no other name for it than 'hooked mat.' But it was, and is, a thousand things besides."

IV

BACK TO THE OLD DYE KETTLE

THE women of early Colonial times produced their dyes from the materials about them, and huge brass or copper kettles for dyeing were part of each household's outfitting. It seems particularly appropriate that in making woven coverlets and hooked rugs, or in any of the old-time handicrafts, Colonial dyes should be used for coloring. It's a true adventure to work with them, and I really wish to urge you to make use of them. You might have the delightful experience of discovering something new, as did an Indian-basket maker who "found in the purple iris a dye almost as deep as its own blossoms."

The art of dyeing needs a volume by itself, and I can give only a few suggestions to point out the path of old-time coloring.

Of course you know that you need a mordant to fix or set the dye. Wood-ash alkali was used by the ancients, and Colonial craftswomen used alum, cream of tartar, sal ammoniac, verdigris, and copperas. Alum is practical because it is so easily obtained. Different recipes are given for mixing the mordant; one of the best is three ounces of alum dissolved in a quart of water.

A few of the ingredients named in these pages are poisonous, and should be handled with precaution. Others have unpleasant effects on the skin. It is always safer to handle wet dyed stuffs with a pair of forked sticks.

YELLOW

The stems, leaves, and flowers of St.-John's-wort give a pleasing yellow color; yellow can likewise be made from walnut, hickory, yellow oak, and Lombardy-poplar barks, also from tumeric, peach leaves, smartweed leaves, sumac stalks, and clematis, or from alder and birch barks. Onion skins produce a dull yellow, and saffron, purchased at the drug store, makes a bright yellow.

RED

Cochineal is a preparation made from the bodies of minute insects fed upon cactus plants. It was always included in Grandmother's dyeing supplies. It was long used by the Indians of Mexico, but was not introduced into Europe until after the Spanish conquest. From cochineal a dark, deep red dye is made. When combined with cream of tartar, a bright red is produced.

Madder grows in the South, and its root is used to make a dull red dye. New England rug-makers can purchase it in powder form at the drug store. The plant is a native of India and northeastern Asia, and for many hundreds of years raising it was one of the principal occupations of certain people of Asia Minor. Its chief coloring principle, now known as alizarin, was familiar to ancient peoples; both Pliny and Herodotus mention it. Cloth colored with alizarin has been found on ancient Egyptian mummies.

A purplish red is obtained from pokeberry root. Cranberries and beets give a dull red.

Gertrude DeWager mentions an interesting fact in regard to a certain pink dye used in Colonial times: "Attar or otto, an irregular, delicate pink or flesh tint, was made from pink dust obtained by scraping soft bricks. In Colonial times it was no uncommon task for women to scrape the inside brick walls of tombs to obtain this dust. With the dye made from it they colored white homespun cloth for quilt linings."

BLUE

One of the best-known blues is made from indigo. It is one of the most ancient dyes, and its native home is in India. In fact, the word comes from the Latin name, *indicum*, and this in turn from *Indicus*, meaning Indian. It will not dissolve in water, so sulphuric acid must be used with it. To prevent rotting of the stuff to be dyed, neutralize by the addition of soda before putting the material in the dye bath. Pour the acid, drop by drop, upon the indigo, stirring all of the time with a long stick. The liquid will foam. Just as soon as the indigo is dissolved, add water, and then turn in soda until it stops foaming.

Spiderwort flowers, wax myrtle, garden purslane, and larkspur also furnish blue coloring matter.

GREEN

Green can be produced by combining yellows and blues in different proportions, but Grandmother also knew the value of black-oak bark, and of gold seal combined with indigo, to make green.

ORANGE AND BROWN

The powdered form of dragon's blood gives a rich

orange, and the barks of butternut, hemlock, and maple trees produce shades of brown.

BLACK

Black can be made from bugleweed and logwood. Logwood is obtained from the heartwood of a tree growing in Central America. The dye is made by boiling the fine chips. It was introduced into Europe by the Spaniards.

When is the best time to gather native vegetable materials for dye-making, you will ask? Most authorities agree that October or November harvesting will give the finest results, for then the seeds are fully ripened.

There is an art in the actual dyeing process that comes only by experimentation. Just how much bark or other material to use, is the question. One authority says, "Butternut bark, walnut shucks, sumac, pokeberries, onion skins, and so on — all that can be held in both hands; a little more will do no harm."

As Amy V. Richards says in "When the Clock Reel Ticked" (published in the *Modern Priscilla*), "If, like so many of us, you are seized with the desire to have your coverlets 'just like the old ones,' perhaps you will ask Aunt Genevy how she dyes that rich cream-color.

"'Jest take a few pieces of bark an' throw in,' she will answer.

"'Yes, but how much bark?' you will interrupt her.

"'Jest a few pieces, an' you — '

"'But how much?' you persist.

"'My Gawd, you cain't dew it naow-haow,' promptly closes the interview."

Before the actual dyeing process came the mordanting; then the dyeing in a huge brass kettle, either hanging over the fire or built in at the side of the fireplace. The work was completed by removing the pieces of cloth from the bath and hanging them on lines strung up out of doors, where they flapped gayly in the wind until dry.

Modern workers will use an agate kettle and about two ounces of dye to a gallon of water. About one half hour's good boiling will be necessary to make most dyes give their colors, though cochineal needs fully two hours to produce the best results. Strain the dye into the kettle and be sure to have enough liquid to cover the material, which should be wrung out in water before immersion in the dye bath. Always have the dye boiling, and turn the material constantly with two sticks. Boil from fifteen minutes to one half hour, basing the time upon the strength of the color desired. Remove the cloth from the dye bath, and rinse in cold water until the water remains clear.

I was fortunate in recently meeting a woman whose home is in New Brunswick. From her mother and grandmother she had learned the art of old-time dyeing, which is still practised in the locality where she lives. From her I obtained this rule for dyeing (yellow) with onion skins: —

"Mordant the wool with alum and a little cayenne pepper. Let it boil lightly and keep it warm for about six days. Dry the wool, and then boil a quantity of onion skins and cool. Put the wool in the kettle, cover with the dye bath, and boil lightly for one half hour to one hour; then keep warm for a while. Wring out, and wash."

But perhaps I shall best be able to help crafts workers anxious to discover the lore of old-fashioned dyes, by providing a list of traditional recipes. These recipes were collected from various sources. Some of them were found in an old notebook, filled with household rules and directions written in faded ink. They are offered only as a suggestion to the craftswoman who may desire to experiment with the coloring methods of her grandmother's day.

DYE RECIPES FROM GRANDMOTHER'S NOTEBOOK

BEET RED

Use five or six large beets to a gallon of water. Thoroughly wash them and cook in the water until the vegetables lose their color. Strain the liquid through cheesecloth. Dissolve four ounces of powdered alum in two gallons of water, and soak the material to be dyed in this mordant for two hours. Place the beet juice in a kettle on the front of the stove. When it boils, immerse the material and boil for one half hour, turning the material over and over during the process.

CRANBERRY RED

Boil one pound of cranberries in a gallon of water until they lose color. Continue as with Beet Red.

COCHINEAL SCARLET

Make a bag of cotton cloth and place in it two ounces of cochineal (grain). Tie a string about the mouth of the bag. Place in a stone crock and cover with cold water. After the coloring matter is drawn out, fill a dye pot half full of cold water and add to the cochineal four ounces of oxalic acid, four ounces single muriate of tin, and one ounce of cream of tartar. Boil these ingredients for ten minutes. Fill the kettle with cold water. Thoroughly wet the goods to be dyed, and place in the kettle. (This rule differs from others in that the dye bath is *not* boiling when the material is first immersed.) Bring the contents of the kettle slowly to a boil. It will take about three quarters of an hour. Boil hard for an hour, stirring frequently. Take out the goods and rinse in cold water.

BRIGHT RED

This recipe will dye six or seven pounds of rags. Soak two and one half pounds of redwood chips overnight in a brass kettle. The next morning add one half pound of powdered alum, and boil to obtain the strength of the chips. Strain the liquid. Add the material to be dyed, and simmer until of the desired shade.

MADDER RED

Mordant the goods to be dyed by dissolving five ounces of alum and three ounces of cream of tartar in enough water thoroughly to cover all the material. Bring the contents of the dye kettle to a boil, and boil for one half hour. Then air the material. Return to kettle and boil one half hour longer. Empty the kettle and fill with clean water. Put in one peck of bran. Heat to the warmth of milk, and let the liquid stand until the bran rises. Skim off the bran and put in one half pound of powdered madder. Heat slowly; strain, and return liquid to dye pot. Put in the material and boil for three quarters of an hour. Wash in strong suds, rinse thoroughly, and dry.

CLARET

Water, three gallons; cudbear, twelve ounces; logwood, four ounces; old fustic, four ounces; alum, one half ounce. Boil the goods in it for one hour. Wash and rinse. This will dye from one to two pounds of material.

CRIMSON

These ingredients will dye one pound of goods. Mordant goods in four ounces of powdered alum, dissolved in two gallons of water for two hours. Boil together, in one gallon of water, three ounces of paste cochineal, two ounces of bruised nutgalls, and one fourth ounce of cream of tartar. It will take ten minutes. Strain. Return liquid to dye pot, add mordanted goods, and boil for one hour. Wash, rinse, and dry.

SALMON

Combine one fourth pound of annatto, one fourth pound of scraped soap, and one gallon of water. Rinse the goods well in warm water, immerse in dye bath, and boil hard for one half hour. This will dye one pound of goods.

Straw Color

Peach leaves for dyeing may be gathered at any time of year, but they give a better color in the fall. The dye is made by soaking two quarts of peach leaves in a gallon of water overnight. In the morning let the dyestuff come quickly to a boil, as overboiling gives a brown instead of the desired yellow shade. Place the mordanted material (see Beet Red) in the dye bath, and boil for about one half hour.

Yellow Quercitron

Quercitron comes in the form of a paste. Place two ounces in a cotton bag and soak overnight in water. Dissolve one fourth pound of washing soda in one gallon of water. Immerse the goods to be dyed, and let stand overnight. In the morning fill the dye kettle with four gallons of water and bring to a boil. Pour in the quercitron juice. Place the soaked goods in the kettle and boil for one half hour.

Rich Yellow

Work five pounds of goods in a boiling dye bath with three ounces of bichromate of potash and two ounces of alum, for one half hour. Remove the goods, drain, and cool. Make another bath by dissolving five pounds of fustic in water enough to cover the goods. Boil for one half hour. Wash out and dry.

Iron Buff

Thoroughly dissolve one half pound of copperas in two gallons of warm water. Also dissolve one pound-package of soap powder in two gallons of water. Place the crocks containing these two liquids side by side. Then, using two wooden sticks, place strips of material to be dyed in the copperas solution, taking care that every part of the goods is covered. Remove from the copperas bath and drain. Using the wooden sticks, place the material in the soap-powder solution. Remove and drain. Repeat this process three times. At first a dull greenish yellow will appear, but after the strips of goods are hung to dry out of doors the color will turn from a greenish to a reddish yellow.

Yellow-Orange

Dragon's blood may be purchased from the druggist in either stick or powdered form. As alcohol must be used to dissolve the stick, it is best to buy the powder. Tie two ounces of the powder in a cheesecloth bag and soak overnight in a quart of cold water. In the morning add one gallon of warm water. Let the dye bath come to a boil. The material to be dyed must meanwhile have been mordanted (see Beet Red). Put it in the dye bath and boil hard for one half hour.

Orange

For five pounds of goods use six tablespoonfuls of muriate of tin, and four ounces of argol, with water to cover goods. Boil one hour. Add one teacupful of madder liquid. Boil another half hour.

Wine Color

For five pounds of goods use two pounds of camwood in water to cover well. Boil one half hour, add goods, and boil another half hour. Darken with one and one half ounces of blue vitriol. If not dark enough add one half ounce of copperas.

Sky Blue

Dissolve two ounces of blue vitriol in one gallon of water. Dip goods for fifteen minutes. Rinse in lime water.

Blue (*quick process*)

Cover two pounds of goods in water in which five ounces of alum and three ounces of cream of tartar have been dissolved. Boil for one hour. Then put goods in warm water in which has been dissolved a sufficient amount of extract of indigo to make the desired shade. Boil for one half hour.

Light Blue

Water, one gallon; sulphuric acid, one wineglassful; Glauber salts in crystals, two tablespoonfuls; liquid extract of indigo, one teaspoonful. Boil the goods about fifteen minutes. Rinse in cold water.

Green

Make a dye bath of a pound of fustic and three and one half ounces of alum, with water to cover one pound of goods. Steep until the strength is out and a good yellow is obtained. Remove the chips and add extract of indigo, one tablespoonful at a time, until the desired color is obtained.

Indigo Blue

No list of rules for the use of dyes would be complete without an attempt at describing the making of indigo blue. I have referred to it before, but the details of setting the indigo vat were not given in full. The process needs great care and is beset with difficulties for the amateur dyer. On the other hand, it must be remembered that indigo was one of the most important colors of Grandmother's day, for the shade produced was both beautiful and permanent.

Powdered indigo is very light in weight, and in order to handle it readily, it must be first made into a paste. Mix a pound of powdered indigo with sufficient water to form the paste. Then dilute with about two quarts of water, and turn into a vat placed out of doors. Dissolve two and one half pounds of copperas in boiling water, and then add enough water to cool the liquid. Turn into the vat with the indigo, stirring thoroughly. Mix three pounds of slaked lime with ten quarts of water, and turn into the vat, using a wooden rake for stirring. Now add twenty-four quarts of water. There will now be about forty-four quarts of liquid in the vat, and it should be stirred vigorously. Let it stand for forty-eight hours in a moderately warm place. Occasionally the contents of the vat should be vigorously stirred. If the dye turns out well, the liquid will be dark amber in color and will be covered with a dark blue scum, when stirred with the rake. If the liquid is greenish, there is unreduced indigo present, and more copperas is needed; but if it is brownish, more lime is required. Therefore, the dye must always be tested for color.

The process of dyeing the material is as follows: Immerse the goods in the liquid by means of two wooden sticks. Drain. Repeat the process three times. This will be enough usually, but if the color is not deep enough, repeat until the desired shade appears. Rinse thoroughly and dry out of doors.

GREEN

If the goods are to be colored green, dye them with indigo first, then overlay with quercitron yellow.

Manganese Brown

Dissolve two ounces of permanganate of potash in two gallons of warm water. The resulting liquid will be crimson instead of brown in color. With wooden sticks place the damp goods in the liquid, taking care that all parts are covered. Remove from the dye bath. Hang on a line out of doors until the material turns brown. The required shade is obtained by re-dipping, partly drying, and then re-dipping. Dry carefully, wash with soap and hot water, and dry again.

Snuff Brown

For five pounds of cloth use one pound of camwood. Boil it fifteen minutes, then dip the goods for three quarters of an hour. Remove the goods. Add to the dye bath two and one half pounds of fustic. Boil ten minutes, and dip the goods for three quarters of an hour. Add one ounce of blue vitriol and four ounces of copperas. Dip again for one half hour. If not dark enough, add more copperas.

London Brown

This recipe is for three pounds of goods. Boil together for three quarters of an hour three fourths of a pound of camwood, one half pound of logwood, and one ounce of quercitron bark. Add two ounces of copperas, and boil the goods for one half hour. Rinse thoroughly, and dry.

Butternut Brown

Do not boil, but steep hot for half an hour one half bushel of butternut bark. Steep the goods for one hour, and air. Add one ounce of copperas to the liquor and bring it to a boil. Immerse the goods and boil for one half hour. If not dark enough, use more copperas. One part butternut bark and one part black walnut bark make a pleasing color. Experiment in the same way with hemlock bark.

BROWN (*made from scaly moss*)

This is a very old recipe. "The scaly moss from rocks and ledges is a good material for coloring brown. Gather the moss and place it in a brass kettle, upon which pour cold water; then let it boil on the stove for three or four hours. Skim out the moss, put in the goods, and boil until you have the desired color. It will never fade."

CATECHU BROWN

Catechu, which is the dried sap of certain East Indian trees, comes in the form of dried paste. Soak two ounces of the catechu overnight in a stone crock. In the morning put the liquid into the dye kettle with four gallons of boiling water and one ounce of copperas. Immerse the material to be dyed, and boil for one hour and a half. Make a solution of one ounce of bichromate of potash to one gallon of water. Place the goods in this, and allow them to remain for about five minutes. Do not wring the material when you remove it from the solution, but allow it to drip until it dries. Wash and dry again.

DARK TAN

For five pounds of cloth allow one pound of japonica, eight ounces of bichromate of potash, and two table-spoonfuls of alum. Dissolve the japonica and alum in enough water to cover the goods. Wash the goods in suds and place in the dye. Let the contents of the dye kettle stand for two hours at scalding heat, then set aside until morning. In the morning remove the goods from the kettle. Dissolve the bichromate of potash in water to cover the goods. Put in the goods. Bring the dye bath to scalding heat, and allow it to remain at that temperature for an hour.

LIGHT TAN

Soak two quarts of sumac leaves and one quart of stems overnight in a gallon of water. In the morning boil for one half hour. Add mordanted material (see Beet Red). Boil for three quarters of an hour. Wash the goods and dry.

NANKEEN

This is a very old recipe. "Fill a five-pail brass kettle with small pieces of white birch bark and water. Let it steep (but do not boil) for twenty-four hours. Then skim out the bark. Wet the cloth in soapsuds; then put it in the dye, stir well, and air often. When dark enough, dry. Then wash in suds. It will never fade."

DRAB

For five pounds of goods use one fourth of a pound of green tea and two tablespoonfuls of copperas. Tie the tea in a cloth and steep in a brass kettle. Then add the copperas and skim thoroughly. Put in the goods, and stir and air until colored enough. Rinse and dry.

PURPLE

For each pound of goods to be dyed use two ounces of cudbear. Wet the goods well in soapsuds. Then dissolve the cudbear in hot suds, not quite boiling, and soak the goods until of the required color. The color is brightened by rinsing in alum water.

BLACK

Dissolve three fourths of an ounce of bichromate of potash in three gallons of water. Boil the goods in this for forty minutes; then wash in cold water. Add nine ounces of logwood extract, three ounces of fustic, and one or two drops of double oil of vitriol to three gallons of water. Boil for forty minutes. Rinse in cold water. Dry. This will color from one to two pounds of goods.

Possibly you are one of the crafts workers who believes that the day of the old-time dyes is past, and that you cannot give the time and the effort to perfect the somewhat tedious art of your grandmother's era. In that case, you will make use of some of the several varieties of commercial dyes for coloring the materials of your hooked rugs.

Commercial dyes, as well as the coloring matter used by the women of old New England, have their romance, and any student of chemistry can relate interesting details in regard to the discovery of aniline dyes. I will tell of but one, the discovery of mauve. Briefly, it is this. In 1856 William Henry Perkin, while attempting to obtain artificial quinine from coal tar, produced a queer black mass which caused him great disappointment. But to his astonishment, the black mass, when placed under water, turned to a lovely purplish color. So was born mauve, the first of the aniline dyes.

Dyeing calls for careful work and attention to detail. It is best not to have the cloth in too large pieces. Some workers cut it in three-yard lengths, saying that it is easier to handle, and that the material is not so greatly wasted. This, of course, is for new cloth. Scraps from the piece bags or worn household materials and clothing must be used in the most convenient form.

All commercial dyes contain directions for the amount of dye used in proportion to the material. For this reason the goods must be weighed while dry, and the directions carefully followed.

The best utensils for boiling dyes are made of copper or brass, or the more modern granite or porcelain. There are chemical reasons why it is inadvisable to use iron and tin. The kettle should be of sufficient size to allow the materials to be completely immersed in the dye bath while boiling. The worker should also provide herself with two clean forked sticks with which to handle the material in the bath, and a vessel of some sort for rinsing the dyed fabrics.

The material must be thoroughly wet before placing it in the dye bath. Helen Albee says that when she dampened her materials she plunged them into scalding water and dipped them up and down with two sticks. When flannel, for example, was thoroughly soaked, and no white spots remained, she lifted it from the hot water and laid it aside to cool before immersing in the dye bath.

If you wish your material to be uniform in color, all of it should be immersed at the same time. If, however, you desire a slight variation in tone, which really will make your rugs more interesting, try dipping the cloth in parts, one piece at a time.

There are a few details in regard to dyes which a crafts worker must know. First, *follow directions*. In all cases, the kind of mordant called for should be used, and the dye bath should be carefully strained before the materials are immersed. I once saw a linen dress completely ruined because the owner had hurried and had not thought it necessary to strain the dye bath. One expert rug-maker tells me that she always adds a little black to all of the colors to take off — as she expresses it — the too vivid effect of the raw dyes. This same worker also offers the suggestion of boiling extremely bright colored material in strong soap suds to refine and mellow it.

Any worker who has the least knowledge of color knows that the three primary hues can be combined to make the secondary. It seems a little like kindergarten work to mention the fact here that blue and yellow make green, red and yellow make orange, and red and blue make purple. Martha Jane Phillips adds further information by saying:—

Red + yellow   = yellow-red
Yellow + green = green-yellow
Green + blue   = blue-green
Blue + purple = purple-blue
Purple + red   = red-purple

These principles of color combination should be

remembered when dyeing cloth other than white, ivory, light gray, and pale tones of other colors. Anyone who has watched different colored materials emerge from the same dye bath knows that wide variations may be caused by — say — placing yellow cloth or blue cloth along with white in a red dye bath.

Light tones of strong colors may be made by using less dye than that called for in the directions. For instance, lilac is made by using about one fourth of the regular amount of deep purple, when dyeing over white cloth.

The temperature of the dye bath when the goods are placed in it should be hot, but below the boiling point, for if the bath is too hot the cloth will become spotted. The cloth should be entirely covered by the liquid, and it must be stirred during the entire time that it is in the bath. No part should float on the top of the dye bath or remain at the bottom. The dye bath is finally raised to just the boiling point or a little below, and kept at that temperature for at least twenty minutes longer. The material is then removed and rinsed in several waters until the water is perfectly clear, and the process is completed by hanging the cloth on the clothesline to dry.

V

JUST HOW TO MAKE A HOOKED RUG

MAKING hooked rugs is a process of real handwork. Each stitch must be pulled through a mesh of the background, one stitch at a time. On first thought the idea may seem tedious to the worker who contemplates rug construction, but she will become encouraged as she progresses and finds that practice in the art gives her facility in handling her rug hook. There is no reason why any woman who has patience and is at all successful in the use of her hands cannot make a hooked rug for use in her own home, or possibly to sell.

The working materials needed are background fabrics, bits of cloth or worsteds for pulling in, dyes of various hues for coloring the filling materials, a set of wooden frames to hold the burlap, a steel rug hook, and, if desired, a simple rug machine. The use of the rug machine raises the question of whether or not you wish your finished product to be a purely handmade object. I know workers who would never think of using a machine of the most simple type, and I know others who always use one for filling in backgrounds.

Let us talk a little about the background materials. As I have said in a previous chapter, our foremothers used homespuns, linsey-woolseys, linens, and, later, cotton cloth for the foundations of their rugs. Still later, when gunny sacks for grains and potatoes came into use, the New England housewife, with her usual Yankee thrift, washed the bags, pressed them, and used them for foundation material. The modern worker buys heavy jute burlap of a good quality and an even mesh. She purchases it from art stores, from dry-goods stores, or from the mail-order houses. Forty inches is the best width. She cuts it to the required size, hemming the ends to prevent fraying.

And now, if you are the worker in question and have purchased a stamped pattern for your rug, all well and good. The foundation needs only to be placed in the frames. If you are a creative worker and wish to make your own design, there are various methods employed in drawing it. One elderly woman told me that she had seen her grandmother withdraw a charred stick from the fire, drop it in a basin of cold water and then use it to mark off her design. I have seen rug-makers use small brushes dipped in ink, or even sticks dipped in liquid bluing or ink; and one up-to-date young woman uses dark blue or black crayons for drawing her simple, freehand patterns.

Stencils are satisfactory to transfer corners and ends. A fourth of the rug pattern should be drawn, then a stencil made, and the pattern applied to the other three quarters. Place the stencil so that the edge follows a thread, and fasten it in position with pins or tacks. Fill in the opening of the pattern with liquid bluing, applied with a stiff brush.

One of the earliest methods of drawing rug designs was by the use of the paper pattern. Patterns of leaves, simple flowers, and scrolls were cut, and rug-makers exchanged patterns of a graceful scroll or a rose-and-leaf design as their descendants exchange ideas for parchment lampshades. If you follow the idea of the paper pattern, you should use lightweight cardboard for the final motif to be traced. You can experiment with paper at first to get just the idea you need, but after you have made a successful pattern, transfer it to the more durable cardboard. I was once shown a rug bearing the picture of a stiff-legged horse. The woman who made it was the wife of a local horseman and she had made the rug for her eldest son. She told me that she cut the pattern of the animal from paper exactly as a child cuts paper dolls.

Conventional patterns are easy to make. Bricks can be used, as they were in Grandmother's day, to mark off tiles; plates bring out a pattern quite Eastern in effect; and diamond patterns are easily managed by using a yardstick for the long intersecting lines. If you have a little talent for freehand drawing, you can create a pattern for a "wall" rug as did a northern New Hampshire worker who hooked a picture of the Old Man of the Mountain upon burlap.

In all cases it is necessary to find the centre of your background before applying the design, and this is done by drawing diagonal lines from one alternate corner to the other. The intersection of the lines will give you the central point.

Whatever method of pattern-making you employ, always lay the burlap out as smoothly as possible upon the table and hold it in place by tacking at the corners.

Sew your rug foundation into the frames, to hold the work straight and true during the hooking-in process. Any cabinetmaker or Jack-of-all-trades can make you a set of frames, and the local blacksmith can make a rug hook. Frames and hook may also be purchased from firms dealing in handicraft supplies. I will describe a set of frames. The set is made from soft wood and consists of four pieces, each two inches wide and one inch thick. The side pieces are four feet long; half-inch auger holes, three inches apart, are bored along the middle of the strips, near the ends. The crosspieces are about a foot and one half long, and each one has placed, one and one half inches from the end, a fixed peg of such a size that it will fit easily into the auger holes. By inserting the pegs in the auger holes, a rectangular frame is formed, and you will see that it can be readily adjusted to various-sized rugs. To keep the frames square and true, a twelve-inch strip should be nailed on each of the crossbars and fitted in such a way as to come out flush against the lengthwise pieces when the frames are put together.

Less elaborate frames are made of four strips of wood, wound with cloth and held together at the corners with steel clamps, which may be purchased at any hardware store.

The rug hook somewhat resembles a crochet hook, and either it is set in a wooden handle or the end is bent and wound with a piece of cloth. Different workers use different hooks, and only experience can teach you the kind best adapted to your hands. There are two things to remember, however: too small a hook will catch in the work, and too large a hook will make unsightly spots in the burlap. If you wish to have a hook made at the blacksmith's, ask him to try a nail about a fourth of an inch in thickness, filed into shape at the end, and bent slightly. Have him set this in a wooden handle.

You should use heavy white twine and a darning needle for sewing the burlap into the frames. This is one of the most important steps in rug-making, as the perfect shape of the completed product depends upon the care taken in this step. I know of one worker who spends an entire afternoon in putting the rug in the frames. She sews it in by wrapping the twine about the sides of the frames and pulling it through the edges of the burlap. This woman always attaches the shorter ends first, smoothing and pulling the burlap until it is taut and true. If you are using the cloth-wound frames, sew the twine through the cloth, then back again into the burlap. Other crafts-women do not sew their foundation into the frames, but tack it on the strips of wood. If this method is used, the burlap is doubled along the edges, in order that the tacks may not pull out threads in a single thickness. An inch border of plain burlap should be left outside of the pattern, as you will find it difficult to hook close to the edges of the frames.

Now comes the selection of the material to be used in hooking in the pattern. Flannel is perhaps the best choice. Chenille is excellent; the background of one of the prettiest rugs that I have ever seen was hooked in with strips cut from old chenille portières. A worker recently called my attention to the waste ends which can be bought at a certain price per pound from mills making sweaters. Many of the colors are pleasing and the materials pull in well. In fact, almost any lightweight goods like serge, woolen underwear, and even stockings may be used. Broad-cloths and coatings are out of the question, as it is impossible to cut them fine enough to be pulled in. Yarns and worsteds give pleasing results and, since no cutting is required, they save time for the worker. Old hand-knitted sweaters and scarves may be un-raveled and hooked in. In fact, no bit of woolen cloth of the desired weight need be wasted or rele-gated to the old-clothes man if you once start making

Courtesy of South End House Industry, Boston

WORKER AT FRAMES.   NOTICE THE METHOD OF SEWING RUG INTO THE FRAMES

rugs; and I have heard a man, whose wife was interested in the craft, declare that she was cutting up his perfectly good trousers!

When you are ready to commence work, place your frames in a horizontal position across the backs of four chairs or across two tables, at a height comfortable for you. Much of the tediousness of the work can be avoided by taking the right position.

The cutting of the cloth is most important. Cut in straight narrow strips perhaps a fourth of an inch in width. This width is not always infallible, and the best way to do is to experiment a little, making the strips fine enough to pull easily through the meshes of the burlap. After a little practice you will find that, with a pair of sharp scissors, you can prepare the material rapidly. One worker always cuts her strips in the evening so they will be ready for the next day's work, but she is a professional rug-maker and feels for business reasons that she must make every minute count.

Hold the strips of cloth or strands of worsteds to be pulled in between the thumb and forefinger of the left hand, placed underneath the burlap foundation, and draw the loops through the meshes by means of the hook held in the right hand. The strips should not be too long, and both ends should be brought to the right side. You can use your own taste about the height of the loops, but many experienced workers pull them through to one fourth of an inch or three eighths of an inch in height. Pull the loops closely together, but not near enough to give a hard appearance to the rug. There are one or two "tricks of the trade." Drop the hook below the strip and pull it upwards instead of winding the strip about the

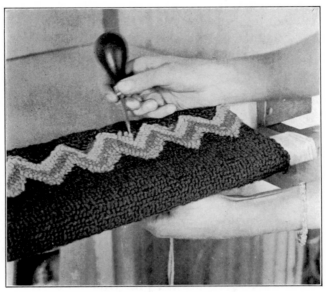

Courtesy of the Massachusetts Normal Art School
HOLDING THE HOOK AND THE MATERIAL TO BE DRAWN IN

hook. As you draw the loop through, keep the hook almost horizontal, and press against the back of the hole with the smooth side. This prevents the hook from catching in the meshes of the burlap. After a little practice the loops can be pulled through the burlap very quickly, and there is a certain swing in doing it which enables the worker to make the loops both quickly and evenly.

The outline of the pattern should be hooked first. This should be carefully done, and the filling of the design should not be crowded as the work progresses. After the design is filled in, hook the background, taking care that all corners shall be carefully filled. Old-time workers often filled their backgrounds zig-zag instead of straight back and forth, and this method gave a pleasing texture. New colors or shades should be mingled by broken lines, placing the end of one line a little above the end of the other. All these directions apply to one section of the rug.

Experienced rug-makers pull in the design and the background of a small part of the rug and, when this is completed, roll up the rug as the work progresses. This is not necessary in making a small rug, and a small rug is the one for the amateur to attempt first. Do not be discouraged if you make a mistake, for if a line of stitches is poorly done the loops may be pulled out without disturbing the rest of the pattern; and if you are not sure of liking a color in a certain place, some may be hooked in for an experiment and removed if the effect is not pleasing.

You can leave your loops as you pulled them through or you can clip them. This last method gives a chenille appearance to the rug, which is greatly admired by some people. I have been told that the early New England hooked rugs were unclipped and that sheared rugs are of a later period. In clipping, use very long sharp scissors and cut with even strokes, taking off the merest trifle from the tops of the loops. Great care should be used, as poor clipping may easily spoil the product of long hours of hooking.

Remove the finished rug from the frame and cut the burlap evenly on all four sides of the rug, two or three inches from the edge. Turn these edges back, overhanding them or hemming them down securely, so that no part of the burlap edge shows as the rug lies on the floor. If you prefer, you can face back the edges. This method must be followed in making one of the rugs with scalloped edges, to which I referred in a previous chapter. In making round, oval, hexagonal, or octagonal rugs, the shape desired is marked off by two or three rows of hooking and, after the rug is completed and cut out, the edge is carefully faced back. Old-time workers sometimes added a "chenille" strip, made by rolling a length of cloth, or a braid plaited from black or neutral-colored cloth, about the edge of the rug to make it more durable. Some workers line their rugs with cotton cloth or ticking; others leave them as they take them from the frames.

One of the hooked-rug workers of the South End House Industry in Boston told me of an unusual manner of finishing the rugs there, which she assured me is most practical. The burlap is turned back about two inches on the right side, and when the edges of the rug are reached the loops are pulled through both thicknesses of the burlap. This process calls for careful work and judgment in pulling in. It cannot be done so quickly as the other hooking, but, as the worker said, "When it's done, it's done, and we don't have to finish the rug afterward."

The last touch lies in carefully brushing the completed rug with a stiff whisk broom or, if the shearing method was used, in evening the surface with a fine wire brush. You can then press the rug with a warm iron, exactly as you would press a suit of clothes, or lay it on the floor, under another rug, until it stays perfectly flat.

There is one point that I wish to make with the novice in rug-making. Do not let your enthusiasm run away with you so that you confine yourself too closely to the frames. Although pleasant and interesting, the work may become somewhat tiring and rest should be taken from it.

How to Make the Hooked Rug Facing Page 78

I have chosen the hooked rug with the flower-basket design for a lesson in crafts work for two reasons: the design and the coloring are pleasing and artistic, though the rug as a whole is simple enough for an amateur to execute. You won't become discouraged before the work is completed, for the rug is only a yard long and twenty-eight and three quarters inches wide. This is a practical size, too. You will find innumerable places in your house where it will just fit in.

Shall we make-believe, as the children say, that I am sitting with you and offering a few suggestions concerning the making of this little rug? You have purchased a rectangular piece of even-meshed burlap, four inches longer and four inches wider than the completed rug, and have pulled threads by which you have cut it. The rug in the picture is perfectly true, and it is the care used in cutting and sewing into the frames that makes it so.

As I have said, there are various methods of finishing the edges of hooked rugs. Our model rug is a product of the South End House Industry of Boston, and therefore, to use a somewhat mixed way of speaking, was "finished before it was begun." That is to say, the edges on the four sides of the burlap were turned back two inches on the front of the rug and pressed with a hot iron. Let's proceed by that method too, for it will save time in the end. When we hook through both thicknesses of the burlap at the edge, the rug will be completed before we remove it from the frames.

There is something about a basket of flowers in a design that recalls the true spirit of early New England handicrafts, and the pattern in this rug has all the charm and quaintness of the ancient rugs

PLEASING IN DESIGN AND COLORING, THIS RUG IS SIMPLE ENOUGH FOR THE NOVICE TO EXECUTE. DIRECTIONS FOR MAKING IT ARE GIVEN IN THE ACCOMPANYING PAGES

which adorned foreroom floors, and of basket quilts arranged over plump live-goose-feather beds.

The design is so simple that almost anyone who can write can make it, if she carefully studies the picture. The border is three and one quarter inches wide. The design, taken as a whole, is twenty-three inches across the widest part and seventeen inches in height. First, we must make a pattern for the basket, which has a base eight and one half inches wide and a top eleven inches wide. It is six inches high. Block it roughly upon a piece of paper. Then cut it out, shaping it with the scissors as you cut. Choose a piece of heavy brown wrapping paper, the size of the rug inside the border. Indicate the upper line of the lower border, and place the basket pattern two and three quarters inches above it.

As you study the picture, you will notice that five of the flowers are circular in shape. Cut paper patterns for them. The flower at the right of the basket is three and three quarters inches wide, and the one above it is three inches wide. The flower at the upper left of the design is three and one quarter inches wide. Above the basket are two circular flowers. The lower one is three and one quarter inches wide and the one above it two and three quarters inches. The buds are five inches long and one and three quarters inches wide. The bell-shaped flower at the top is six inches long and two inches wide, and the one on the left is five inches long and three inches wide. The leaves vary a little in size, but not greatly in shape. The larger ones are four and one quarter inches long and the smaller ones three inches long. Cut patterns for the leaves, and arrange them with the flower patterns upon the wrapping paper as they are placed in the picture of the rug. Trace around them, and then draw the stems.

Treat the wrapping paper with a wash of boiled linseed oil and a little japan dryer, applied with a wide brush. Cut out the motifs of the design with a sharp knife, but draw the stems upon the burlap after you have stenciled the motifs.

For the stenciling use liquid bluing and a stencil brush with short stubby bristles. Fasten the burlap firmly with thumb tacks on the top of an old wooden table and tack the stencil upon it. Holding the brush in a vertical position, pat in the bluing, beginning in the centre of the design. When you remove the stencil be sure to lift it straight up, as to let it slide, even a little, blurs the work.

One woman who produces lovely hooked rugs told me of her method of making basket patterns. She buys a piece of cretonne with a basket in the design, cuts out the selected motifs, including the basket, and, placing them upon the burlap, traces around them with a carpenter's pencil.

The tools for making hooked rugs have already been discussed in this book. If you study the photograph of the worker at the frames on page 71 you will understand exactly how the burlap is sewn into them. You might easily spoil a good rug by lack of care in this step. Re-read the directions previously given (page 73).

Our model rug is made of all-wool flannel. The material was purchased in its undyed state and colored to suit the taste of the designer. The border is indigo blue, with three rows of dark blue on the edge of the rug and two rows of black on the inner border line. The background is soft fawn, and the basket is in shades of rich brown. The circular flower at the right of the basket and the one in the upper left portion of the design are worked in shades of rich blue with yellow centres. The circular flower on the upper right and the bell-shaped flower at the left are worked out in shades of purple. The two flowers above the basket and the buds are lovely "pinky" orange, while the bell-shaped flower at the top is deep yellow. Great care was used in selecting the greens for the model rug, and I suggest that you experiment with your dyes until you get deep harmonious shades of this color.

Whether you use homemade or commercial dyes, experiment with your colors and always make notes of the results for later reference. You will find such notes of untold value if you continue in the work. Look over the color directions in the book and those that come with dye packages. Select those that seem to meet your requirements and then try them.

To vary the intensity of the colors, New England housewives sometimes wrapped parts of the goods to be dyed in corn husks before immersing in the dye bath, and the method is not to be scorned by modern workers.

For your first attempt at rug-making, do not cut your rags too fine. The flannel strips in the model rug were cut about one half inch in width. You will find that strips of this size will pull in easily and fill in rapidly.

Of course you will see at once that more material will be needed for the background than any other part of the design. If we use new flannel, one yard in width, we must provide two and one half yards for the background; one and one half yards for the blue border; one fourth of a yard for the brown basket; one fourth of a yard for the black edge inside the border and for the accenting of the flowers; one half yard for each of the two shades of green with which the leaves are worked; and one fourth yard for each of the colors shown in the flowers. If we are not buying new goods for the rug, but are picking up odds and ends around the house in thrifty New England style, we shall need more material and must allow half again as much filling as we have outlined.

Now that the design is stenciled upon the burlap, the rug stretched like a quilt in its frames, and the material for pulling in is dyed the right shades, you are ready to begin the actual work of hooking in.

You have spent a day in drawing the design and sewing the rug into the frames and another in coloring the goods, and I know that you are anxious to see the work begin to grow.

Place the frames over the backs of four chairs, as already suggested, or from one table to another, or rest them across light carpenter's horses at a height convenient for you to work easily. Turn to the picture of the rug hook and the method of pulling the burlap through the canvas on page 74. In our model rug, the loops are hooked in one half inch above the foundation.

This rug is so small that it can be hooked without rolling. First work the basket, using at least three shades of brown. Make the outline of the basket and a zigzag strip across it of the darkest shade. Blend the two lighter shades in the body. Work the blue flowers in three shades of blue. You can use up the lighter blues of the border for them. Two shades of purple are used in the bellflower, with the lighter shade in the centre. The yellow bellflower has only one tone value, but is relieved by the deep green of the calyx. Two shades are used in the lower pinky-orange flower, but the upper one has a yellow centre with two rows of the pinky orange on the outside.

After you have completed the flowers, work the leaves, then the stems. The background is pulled in next, and the hooking is completed by making the border. You will find it a little more difficult to pull through the two thicknesses of the border than to hook the design and groundwork, but "when it's done, it's done," and the finish is neat and pleasing. When your last loop is pulled through, remove the rug from the frames. Place a damp cloth on the wrong side and press with a hot iron. Your rug, a real treasure, to be handed down to your daughter and your daughter's daughter, is completed.

VI

COLLECTING HOOKED RUGS

THE Lover of Hooked Rugs, his wife, and I were at a country auction in a tiny New Hampshire town on the Connecticut River. A throng of people, inhabitants of surrounding villages, summer residents, and the ever present collectors of antiques, watched with interest as the auctioneer held up a perfectly made, carefully preserved, old-time hooked rug.

A number of the spectators desired that treasure, and the bidding went rapidly on. Finally the Lover of Rugs, with a grin of delight, wrote out a check, and the prize was ours to examine at our leisure.

It seemed absurd that anyone should presume to walk upon that thing of beauty! Upon a background the color of cream skimmed from a pan of Jersey milk, was a wreath of old-fashioned posies, pulled in with colors of exquisite hue. A black "endless chain" — which the new owner told us proudly added to its value — formed a border. The colors were softly mellowed; the design was simple, yet satisfying; the work was carefully done, as finely executed as a bit of Spanish tapestry. The texture of the rug was as soft as Lyons velvet. It was a splendid specimen of the kind of rugs made by our great-grandmothers.

The hooked-rug mania is sweeping the country with as much spirit as the interest in early American glass! You have only to try to collect rugs to find out how everybody is looking for them. Gone is the day when a well-made specimen could be unearthed at any country auction, or purchased for the proverbial song from the white-aproned mistress of some outlying farmhouse. A notice of a country auction inserted in the local paper will bring collectors and antique-dealers from miles around. Oh, yes, I know, you may be one of the exceptional persons who boast of luck in "picking up" a rug. You *are* exceptional!

If you are collecting hooked rugs, you are collecting for one of a number of reasons: either you have started a collection of genuine antiques and wish to add to it; you are collecting them because you are interested in all forms of old American handicraft; you are collecting because your best friend is, and you don't wish to be outdone; you are collecting just because you simply love the charm and quaintness of the rugs themselves; or you are working to get the right color note in some room, or to match your chintz hangings.

If you are a collector of the last sort, you can get exactly what you desire from any of the well-known designers or you can make rugs yourself. If you are the first kind of collector, only poking about in nooks and crannies and unearthing your finds yourself will meet your needs — that is, of course, unless you have a fat and portly pocketbook, when your dealer may find wonderful specimens for you. Then part of your joy is gone.

Courtesy of "The House Beautiful"

EVEN ON THIS HOOKED RUG OWNED BY MRS. MARY PERKINS TAYLOR, "THE ANIMALS WENT IN TWO BY TWO!"

Courtesy of "The House Beautiful"

UNUSUAL, INDEED, ARE HOOKED-RUG DESIGNS IN WHICH WIDE-SKIRTED DAMSELS, BOYS IN ROUNDABOUTS, AND PERKY POODLES ENJOY THE SEA BREEZES, AS IN THIS RUG OWNED BY MRS. MARY PERKINS TAYLOR

Usually it is inheriting a hooked rug made by your grandmother or great-grandmother that starts you collecting. Perhaps at first you did n't quite realize the value of your heirloom, when along came an enthusiastic friend and pointed out the error of your ways.

A woman living in New York wrote me of such an experience with a hooked rug: "As a child, I remember that this rug lay before the outside kitchen door to protect our linoleum," she said. "After my marriage it was rescued from our garage one Sunday through a friend of ours who is a connoisseur of rugs, and who remarked to my husband, 'Does your wife know you have that out here?' It had been placed up behind the seat of our little open roadster, for the comfort of the beloved Irish terrier who always accompanied us on our drives.

"'Reddy' no longer rides on a hooked rug!"

I have heard many interesting stories concerning the curious places in which collectors have discovered such rugs. A woman found three rolled away under the eaves in an old attic where she had been allowed to rummage. The owner remembered that these rugs were taken up when the parlor carpet was purchased. One day, while driving on a back road in a New Hampshire town popularly nicknamed "Bungy," a lover of antiques met a man with a basket of apples in the back of his wagon, and over the apples was thrown a somewhat worn but beautiful rug. Then

and there she stopped him, and a business trans-
action took place which made her the owner of the
covering of that basket.

Country antique shops offer an opportunity for
finding rugs, and once in a while a visit to a farmhouse will disclose a rug which the owner is willing
to sell. A friend of mine conceived the idea of
inserting notices in remote country papers to the
effect that he was looking for hooked rugs. He
received all kinds: some old, some new, some beautiful, some crude. Out of the many sent, however,
he found but four that met his needs.

"Just what shall I look for in hooked rugs, when
I am collecting?" you ask. Age, beauty of design
and craftsmanship, and good condition of the rug
are some of the qualities sought. I have already
told you of the method of estimating age by the
foundation material. Designs will tell you something.
You will soon learn to judge by experience. I spoke
of the unclipped rugs as being older than the sheared.
That is not an infallible rule, however, for many
modern workers use old methods. If the rug's colors
were produced by vegetable dyes, it is usually safe
to say that it is quite old. The old dyes are easy to
distinguish: you can always tell butternut brown.

While speaking of coloring, I might mention a fact
told me by one collector. She bought a beautiful
old rug of which she was very proud, but, to her
dismay, found upon examination that it had been

THIS OLD NEW HAMPSHIRE RUG OWNED BY MRS. OSCAR L. YOUNG IS DECORATED WITH GAY PARROTS, AND IS EVIDENTLY OF HOME DESIGN AS WELL AS OF HOME MANUFACTURE. A DURABLE FINISH IS MADE BY APPLYING A BRAID OF PLAITED FLANNEL

touched up with paints to get the tones desired by the dealer.

The condition of a rug will tell you something of its age, for in many cases, even with the best of care, breaks will be found in the foundation. Don't worry about that, for rugs can be repaired.

The first step in renovating a threadbare rug with ragged edges and unsightly holes is to clean it. This can be accomplished by washing it in lukewarm water, made sudsy with a reliable brand of soap flakes, or it may be sent directly to a professional cleaner. If you use the first method, spread the rug on the ground or upon the floor and scrub it with a stiff floor brush dipped in suds. I have washed much-soiled rugs in a tub of soapy water and rinsed them a number of times in clear baths. The brush-scrubbing method is better, however, unless the rug is very dirty. After the washing process the rug should be hung over a heavy line to dry out of doors.

In many cases the worn part of a hooked rug shows first on the edges. It can be mended by applying eight-inch strips of burlap along the outside of the rug. The strips should be neatly joined until a length long enough to surround the rug is made. The burlap is placed about two inches under the edge of the rug and sewed with heavy thread to the foundation material. The ragged edges of the rug are then cut and felled down upon the new burlap. You must use great care in sewing, and hold the rug so that there shall be no pulling or puckering. If the border has a distinct design, draw the needed lines upon the fresh burlap. Then try to match the colors of the old rug, using dyes if necessary. The hooking in now begins. It is done exactly as described in the previous chapter, except that the rug is not placed in the frames, but held on a table. Hook until within two inches of the edge of the burlap strip, and hem back the edge in the same way that you would finish a new rug. If you find a hole in the centre or other part of an old rug, carefully apply a piece of new burlap to the back, and after trimming the edges of the hole, sew them down upon the patch. Then hook in your design, following the colors closely. Cover the back of the newly hooked part with cloth to make it more durable in both the mended edge and the patch. It may be necessary to clip the loops slightly to make them the same height as those in the original hooking. Pressing with a damp cloth and a hot iron on the wrong side of a mended rug adds to its appearance.

I have sometimes been asked how hooked rugs should be cared for. My answer is, "Use them, but with the same judgment you would display in caring for other articles in your home." Do not shake a hooked rug, — or a braided one either, — but brush it carefully with a stiff whisk broom.

Prices? Oh, I can't tell you that! As with all American antiques, the demand for them sets the

ROSES, LILIES, "PINIES," BLUEBELLS, AND SPRAYS OF LEAVES RUN RIOT ON THIS RUG MADE BY A CRAFTSWOMAN OF BYGONE DAYS

price. It's a question of how badly they are wanted. One New York dealer has told me that at the present time a well-made, beautifully designed hooked rug of rare quality is worth three times as much as an Oriental of the same size. I saw one, some time ago, for which a dealer asked a thousand dollars. Much more than that was demanded for the finest speci-men of antique hooked rug yet discovered. A village woman has sold a rug of the Civil War period for one hundred dollars. I have seen some sold at country auctions for fifty. On the other hand, I found a fairly good old rug in a back-country dealer's shop marked three dollars and fifty cents!

When you have collected your rugs, you will wish to display them. Perhaps you have some that you feel are too valuable to stand the wear and tear of walking upon. Place these upon your walls. They make distinctive decorations. Picture and land-scape rugs are especially charming when treated as wall hangings, and decorators are using modern rugs of this type to add just the right touch to rooms furnished in Colonial style.

VII

BRAIDED OR PLAITED RUGS

Do you remember the inn known as Hornblower's Tavern, which James Boyd describes in *Drums*, his novel of the period of the outbreak of the American Revolution? To the eyes of Johnny Fraser from the North Carolina back-country it was a wonderful place! The boy was especially impressed by his bed-chamber.

"The room was papered in a pattern of roses; the bed canopy and the chair covers were rose-colored chintz; mosquito curtains of fine lawn hung at the windows. A mahogany dresser bore two brass candlesticks and a large mirror; a small carron stove was filled for the summer with paper, fluted in an ingenious design; three oval rag-rugs covered the black-painted floor."

Now, we are not told the nature of these rugs, but I feel confident that they were made of braids or plaits. When sanded floors, swept with hemlock brooms into intricate patterns, gave way to those made of painted spruce and pine boards, housewives began to use up their carefully hoarded bits of cloth by plaiting rugs. The scraps were truly precious, for in days when every piece of fabric was made at home from flax and wool raised on the farm even the smallest pieces were stored away in the attic for future household use.

"How many operations of breaking and bleaching and boiling those home products had to go through before they came out at last as faultless as the fruits of foreign looms!" wrote Ellen H. Rollins in *New England Bygones*. Fabrics so dearly purchased were prized, and quilt-making and rug-making utilized every scrap, both new and old.

Braided rugs are at present having a revival of popularity and, since they are easy to make and to keep clean, modern workers are fashioning them for their floors.

Before actually starting the construction of a braided rug, you should have some practice in making a braid; for, simple as it seems, there is a certain knack in plaiting a firm, even band of cloth. Cut three strips, varying in width from one half inch to one inch, according to the thickness of the material used and the size of the braid desired. Fasten the ends of the strips together neatly with firm stitches and attach them to the covering of a table by means of a safety pin. Now plait the strands as you would braid hair, using great care to keep the raw edges of the cloth inside. You may find it awkward at first, but as you practise you will acquire dexterity in turning the edges and in plaiting evenly. If you do not mind the extra work, you can turn the edges of the strips beforehand and press with a hot iron.

Sometimes you will find an old rug braided with four strands instead of three. This form of plaiting is quite simple. For convenience, number your strands after you have fastened them together, as one, two, three, and four. Pass the second and fourth to the left over the first and third. Then pass the new second to the right over the old second. Repeat until the braid is completed. Five- seven- and even eight-strand braids are made in a similar manner.

You can have your braids of any desired width, but rugs made of small braids are considered more valuable than those constructed in larger widths. Three-quarters-inch braids make pretty rugs.

The choice of material is almost unlimited, for practically any kind of cloth, cotton or woolen, old or new, is suitable. I would n't use cotton and wool in the same rug, however. Rugs made of cretonnes, ginghams, or other firmly woven cotton goods are appropriate for bedrooms and bathrooms, while those made of broadcloths and flannels look well in living-room or hall. Denims are especially good for rugs in summer cottages, as they are durable and artistic and easily cleaned. I have seen lovely braided rugs made of old chenille curtains and from the felting used in paper mills, while short lengths of materials known as mill ends — which can be purchased by the pound from mills manufacturing broadcloth — work up well. Woolen khaki is useful in making braids, for it blends harmoniously with other colors.

You may be able to carry out any color scheme

HANDMADE RUGS ARE USED IN THE ROOMS OF MRS. PARKER WHITTE-
MORE'S HOMESTEAD IN WEST GLOUCESTER, MASSACHUSETTS

your imagination suggests, but an artistic sense in the choice of color is necessary. Perhaps you will like to follow in the footsteps of your grandmother and make an old-fashioned striped three-and-three rug. Translated, this means that three braids, containing similar combinations of color, are sewed together, and that the stripes thus formed are divided from each other by single braids of black or of a dark color.

Let me give you an example. Suppose that you are using yellow and brown for the first stripe of your three-and-three rug. You will make your first braid with one strip of yellow and two of brown, your next with two of yellow and one of brown, and your last braid of three strips of yellow. After you have sewed the three braids together to form a stripe, you will add a black braid, and then start a new stripe with a different color combination. These three-and-three rugs are especially suitable for a room equipped with old New England furniture.

Women in the mountains of New Hampshire make what they are pleased to call "shaded" rugs. As the name tells you, they shade from light centres to dark borders, and only one or two colors are used. You can make artistic rugs of this kind by using brown in its various shades and tints, or combined with dull orange or tawny yellow; shades of green, used alone or with tan and fawn; blue in all its pleasing tones, or combined with gray. Very modern are the rose-and-ivory rugs, or blue ones with gray and black.

Perhaps some definite suggestions in regard to color schemes actually used in braided rugs might be of value. Butternut brown was used for the five central braids of one oval rug. This centre was surrounded by eight braids made of strands of wool khaki, madder red, and gray. Five rows of butternut brown followed, then came eight rows of strands of butternut brown, madder red, and dull green. The rug was finished with four braids of solid dark mahogany.

A round rug was made in alternating dark and light circles. Each circular stripe consisted of four braids, and the colors used were red, green, and gray, separated by black outlines. The centre of another (oval) rug was made of two strands of orange-yellow and one of dull blue. Then came three braids of the blue, two braids of black, and three of blue. These were followed by four braids like the centre; then came a stripe made of the blue, black, and blue braids. In this rug were three stripes braided like the centre and two stripes of the blue, black, and blue braids. Four solid black braids formed the border.

Hooked centres with braided borders are unusual and effective. I have recently seen an antique rug, worthy of being copied, with a centre upon which a quaint nosegay was hooked, while the braided border was made of plaits combining the colors of the

RECTANGULAR BRAIDED RUG MADE IN SHADES OF BROWN AND ORANGE. THE BRAIDS ARE PLAITED
WITH EIGHT STRANDS EACH

centre. The rug was round in shape, and was used in front of a gate-legged table, with a ladder-backed chair standing near it.

The older braided rugs were round. If you wish to make one, you form the centre by coiling a long braid and sewing around and around it in one direction. There is one difficulty in making a rug of this kind, however: unless great care is used, the rug will hoop in the centre and will not lie flat upon the floor. You can eliminate this difficulty by holding the braid loosely as it is sewed.

Oval rugs are the most satisfactory to make. You double and sew together a braid of the required length — sixty inches is a good length — to form the centre of the rug. Now carefully sew on another braid long enough to extend around the centre, and fasten the ends securely on the wrong side. You must use great care in joining these ends, that bunches may not result. Starting in an opposite direction, sew on another braid, and after this sew the braids first one way and then the other. See that the joining of the ends of the braids comes in different spots, or unsightly places will appear on the rug. By cutting each braid to a length extending once around the rug, the work may be kept perfectly flat.

If you decide to make a rectangular-shaped rug, use one straight braid about a yard long for the centre. Then sew on the other braids, first on one

side and then on the other. This method will keep
the rug in perfect shape. After you have sewed all
of the braids, unravel each one for three inches at the
ends and sew securely on the under side to prevent
further fraying. You will now have a rug made of
straight, braided strips, and finished at the ends
with a fringe. If you do not like the fringe, instead
of unraveling the ends of the braids sew four or five
plaits around the sides of the rug for a finish.

In constructing a clover-leaf rug, you make three
small round braided rugs and attach them together
in the form of a clover leaf. Beneath the opening
in the centre sew a piece of burlap which is filled in
by the method I described in making hooked rugs.
Complete by sewing three or four braids around the
entire edge of the clover leaf.

One of the prettiest braided rugs that I have ever
seen was placed before a long bench in the office of
an inn in the White Mountains. It was made of
woolen cloth in shades of gray with touches of dull
red, and I learned afterwards that many pairs of
worn-out Campton trousers went into its construction. You can see, therefore, that it was a purely
New Hampshire product, for the manufacture of
these trousers is to this day an industry of the little
town of Campton in the Pemigewasset valley. The
rug itself was produced by a craftswoman on Sugar
Hill. The braids were small and exquisitely made, but
the outstanding feature of this rug was its unusual

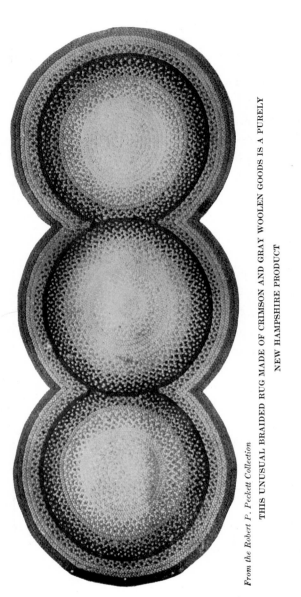

THIS UNUSUAL BRAIDED RUG MADE OF CRIMSON AND GRAY WOOLEN GOODS IS A PURELY

NEW HAMPSHIRE PRODUCT

shape. Three small round rugs were sewed together, side by side, and the whole was finished by sewing seven braids all the way around the attached rugs.

Wheel rugs are interesting. I will tell you how to make one. First construct a centre in the manner described for oval braided rugs. Work the centre out until it is an oval about twenty-seven inches long and twelve inches wide. Then make a number of small braided mats nearly the size of a breakfast plate. Sew them around this centre, and attach the sides of the small mats together. Now sew a border of braids around the outer edge of the combined wheels, carrying the rug out to the desired size. A very beautiful wheel rug has been made in shades of rose, blue, and brown. The last three braids of the border were dark wood-brown.

Panel rugs are made by constructing twenty-inch braided squares, sewing them together, and finishing with a frame of several braids sewed around the edge.

There are two methods that you can use in sewing braids together. One is known as carpet stitch and is done by weaving the thread back and forth between the edges of the braids. A great many workers, however, use the over-and-over stitch, which is simply sewing the edges of the braids together on the under side. In either case you should use very heavy, waxed thread — black or gray — and a medium-sized darning needle. If you wish to make very durable rugs, double the thread before waxing it.

After the rug has grown in size, you will find it impossible during the time at your disposal to sew on more than one braid or possibly two in a day, and for that reason you should keep your work upon a table until it is completed. Placing it upon a table also helps in keeping the work flat.

When your braided rug is finally done, brush it thoroughly and then press with a hot iron. Pressing will give it a finished appearance and also remove any tendency that it may have to hoop. Then, if you have chosen your color scheme with discrimination, braided your strands evenly, and sewed them carefully, you will find that you have produced a piece of handicraft that will give joy to your creative instincts and add to the individuality of your home.

VIII

MADE WITH KNITTING NEEDLES

DIFFERENT nations claim the invention of the art of knitting. We feel quite certain that it was practised in Spain and Italy before it was in England. Knit stockings were little known in England until the time of the great Elizabeth, but we read that during the latter part of her reign the Queen wore stockings made of knitted silk.

Knitting is one of the oldest of American handicrafts. Girls of Puritan and Colonial days made their own stockings, as well as assisting in the manufacture of socks for the entire family. Little children could knit before they could read, and at the dame schools the clack of knitting needles intermingled with the droning of the " A— b — abs" and the couplet,

> In Adam's fall
> We sinned all,

of the old *New England Primer*.

Knitting by hand continued for nearly two hundred years, for knitting machines were not introduced into America until early in the nineteenth century. Numerous fancy stitches, wholly unknown to us, were formerly in use. I was recently shown a pair of lacy white stockings into which a lass of bygone days had knitted her name; and there is a tradition that one enterprising young lady embellished the tops of her stockings with the entire alphabet!

Knitting was an easy way for the housewife to make rugs. All the members of the family — at least, the feminine portion — could be called into service, and I have a fancy that possibly Grandfather too might have passed the long winter evenings before the huge fireplace knitting rug strips on long wooden needles.

Any woman who understands knitting can copy the soft, warm rugs made by her grandmother. There is an old saying to the effect that, some time before she dies, every woman learns to ply knitting needles. Even if this statement is n't literally true, it's a fact that the art has been revived since the beginning of the World War, and that to-day out of ten women nine know how to knit.

Knitted rugs are very nice for bedrooms. I remember visiting in an old New Hampshire farmhouse, years ago, where the guestroom was still called the "spare" room. Here, standing before the tall, plump bed, built up of corn husks and of feathers, and covered with a woven indigo-blue-and-white counterpane, I warmed my poor little cold toes on a hit-or-miss knitted rug. To this day I never see one of these varicolored, homemade rugs without smelling the faint lavender perfume of the linen sheets.

Most simple of all knitted rugs are those made of rags and knit on large wooden needles. Either cotton or woolen rags may be used, but the two are not combined in the same rug. The cloth is cut in strips, varying in width from one quarter to three quarters of an inch. These rags are sewed together just as carpet rags are sewed. Using plain garter stitch, they are knit in strips about six inches wide and of any desired length, and then joined to form a rectangular rug.

In making oval and round knitted rugs, similar kinds of material are used and they are prepared in the same manner. Five stitches are cast on the needles and the strips knit in garter stitch to the required length. In making an oval rug, a centre is formed by shaping a knitted strip about a yard long. When such a strip is doubled and sewed together along the lengthwise edges, the centre is about eighteen inches long. Other strips are then sewed on in exactly the same manner in which braids are sewed on plaited rugs. Round rugs are made in a similar fashion, first sewing the centre around and around, instead of making use of a long strip. These are very pretty when worked out in combinations of gray and blue, rose and ivory, and yellow and tan, while a quaint, old-fashioned effect is achieved by knitting them hit-or-miss.

Unique rugs are made with worsteds knitted on bone needles. Strips about two inches wide and eighteen inches long, of any desired color, are knit in garter stitch. A foundation of old-fashioned pillow ticking — the kind with narrow instead of wide stripes — is cut. The knitted strips are then sewed on both edges over the stripes of the ticking. After all are sewed, each strip is cut through the middle with a sharp pair of scissors, and the result is a surface of fluffy texture. Rugs of this type are frequently completed by sewing three or four braids of woolen cloth about the edges.

Another type of rug is made by knitting strips of woolen cloth on wooden needles and combining these strips with braids, using first a knitted strip of any width, then three or four braids, then another knitted strip, and continuing the work until the rug is completed.

Now let me tell you of a splendid way to use up bits of silks or knitting worsteds by making a "scrappy" knitted rug. Long bone or wooden needles, a ball of heavy white knitting cotton, and a box of silk scraps about an inch and one half long and an inch wide — these are the required materials. Cast on thirty-six stitches and knit once across. On the next row, after knitting two stitches, knit a scrap of silk into the work. Knit two more plain stitches, then knit in another scrap of silk. Continue in this manner until the row is completed. Knit back across plain without any silk scraps; then knit another row, using two plain stitches and the third with the silk scraps, until the rug is of the desired size. Five strips are needed, and usually the rug is square in shape. Hit-or-miss centres with deep black borders are pretty for these. After the strips are sewed together, the whole may be lined with heavy cotton cloth.

The woman who told me how to make these rugs

Owned by Mrs. Mira Goodnow

FLUFFY KNITTED RUG

gave me two tips which I will pass on to you. Sometimes, if your silk material is thin, you will need to knit in two or even three scraps on the same stitch; and if you use worsteds you can knit in three or four different colors at the same time.

But the most artistic and pleasing of all the knitted

rugs are those known by the prosaic name of "wash-board". Old knitted garments may be un-raveled and dyed, or new yarns may be used to make them. Either number twelve or number four-teen steel knitting needles are used. Five or seven stitches — varying with the weight of the yarn — are cast on, and strips twenty-four inches long are knit in plain garter stitch. One hundred and forty-five strips are used for a large rug, but one hundred strips make a good-sized one. Old-fashioned pillow ticking of the kind previously described is used for the foundation. It is cut to the desired size and bound with inch-wide wool braid.

In order that the colors may be readily seen and arranged satisfactorily, all of the completed knitted strips should be hung over a suspended pole or heavy string. From four to six strips of the same color should be knit, that the coloring of the rug may be symmetrical. The knitted strips are sewed over the stripes of the ticking in the manner described for making a fluffy knitted rug. When all of the strips are sewed on, a corrugated or "washboard" appear-ance will be the result. In sewing, the centre strip should be arranged first; then a strip, first on one side and then on the other, until the rug is completed. The corresponding strips on either side of the centre should be of the same colors, and if a wise selection in the shades is made, a rug of real distinction will result.

IX

CROCHETED RUGS

CROCHETING is not so old an art as some of the other forms of handicraft. In a book by Miss Lambert, brought out in 1842 and evidently a reprint of an English publication, entitled *The Hand-Book of Needlework*, are these words concerning crocheting: "Crochet work, although long known and practised, did not attract particular attention until within the last four years, since which time it has been brought to great perfection, and has been applied with success to the production of numerous ornamental works."

This was in 1842, you will notice. We are told that the earliest known use of the crochet needle for lace-making was by the nuns of a convent in Ireland, and that the first piece of filet crochet, a copy of Da Vinci's Last Supper, was made by nuns of the Convent of Mercy near Rouen, France.

It seems a far cry from the dainty roses and shamrocks and the picots of the delicate Irish crochet, made of the finest linen thread, to the crocheted rug made of lengths of cotton cloth, but both belong to the same general family. The materials needed are strips of cotton cloth, a little over a half inch in width and preferably cut on the bias, a large steel or bone (or a medium-sized wooden) crochet hook. Sew your strips as for carpet rags, passing the end of one strip by that of the other and catching

together with a loose stitch or two. I have always
found it best to prepare my material before beginning
the crocheting and to wind it into soft balls. Then
it becomes the best kind of pick-up work when one
spends the afternoon on a neighbor's porch.

Let's imagine that you have decided to crochet a
round rug of old blue, ivory, and rose. Start with a
chain of three, using the old blue, and in the first
stitch make seven single crochet stitches. Crochet
around and around this centre, increasing enough
to keep the work flat and perfectly circular in shape.
If you wish the rug to have a ribbed effect, pick up
the stitches on the back threads. As your rug in-
creases in size, alternate the colors, but finish with
three rows of the dull blue. Fifty rows of crocheting
will make a good-sized rug.

One day, while making a call at a cheerful farmhouse on Sugar Hill, New Hampshire, I noticed some
interesting rugs whose origin I could not at first
determine. I questioned my hostess. They were
crocheted, but were unlike any others with which
I was familiar. The secret lay in the fact that they
were done over "binding twine," a material used on
the farm, which can be purchased at any hardware
store. The method was that used in making Irish
lace over a padding thread. The rugs were widened
in the same manner as the crocheted rug already
described, but the binding-twine padding made them
more firm and durable.

Owned by Mrs. Charles Corey

CROCHETED RUG

Now let me tell you of another attractive crocheted rug that I once saw. It was made of candle wicking! Yes, candle wicking is still to be found, for the revival of tufted bedspreads has led to the manufacture of a material resembling the antique wicking used when candles were run off. This rug was soft and durable, and was dyed a pleasing shade of blue to match the chintz-hung bedroom.

Crocheted rugs can be made by following a filet crochet pattern. You choose a simple pattern and enlarge it upon brown paper. Then, starting with a chain of the desired width and following your pattern, crochet the background of either dark brown, gray, black, or ivory, and fill in the closed blocks of your pattern with any desired color. Finish the rug by crocheting two or three rows around it for a border.

A very attractive rug, a perfect rectangle in shape, is crocheted from half-inch strips of rose and white cotton cloth, and binding twine is used for the foundation thread. You first make a chain about eighteen inches long and, using it as a basis, crochet over the twine, down one side of the chain and up the other. You will find it necessary to widen as you turn, that the rug may lie flat when completed. The corners of the second row are made as follows: Widen three stitches at the side of the turn; crochet two stitches; widen again. Then work down to the turn at the other end of the chain and widen three stitches; crochet two stitches; widen two stitches. On every round, widen three stitches at the turn. Of course you have been working over the binding twine all the time. If you find one side getting a little longer than the other, pull the twine on that side a little tighter. The centre should be made hit-or-miss of the rose and white strips, but the border should be of solid dark rose. The same idea may be carried out in blue and white. In order to have your rug perfectly true, watch your work, and frequently lay it on the floor to see if the sides are even.

Another uncommon crocheted rug, made of narrow strips of cotton cloth in various colors, is formed of small circles crocheted separately and sewed together. To make a circle, chain five and join in a ring. Make a row of single crochets over the ring. Crochet until the circles are as large as bread-and-butter plates, widening as necessary to keep the work flat. Using one circle as the centre, arrange them in rows and join together with rows of black crocheting. Old stockings make excellent black material for this rug.

Firms dealing in handicraft materials are making special heavy cottons for crocheting rugs, so you can carry out almost any idea and color scheme that you have in mind.

Cretonnes and chintzes make crocheted rugs that resemble the Dresden effects of beautiful ribbons.

Jute, the material from which so many popular bags have been made, works into artistic and serviceable crocheted rugs that are suitable for halls, sun parlors, and porches. There are two forms of jute — the rope and the yarn. The rope is heavier and comes in hanks. It is suitable for certain types of hooked rugs and for braided rugs. The yarn jute is soft like wool, but the texture is different; it comes in many beautiful colors.

The prettiest rug of this (jute) type that I have ever seen was placed before the huge outside stone fireplace on a porch in a mountain country home. It was made of natural-colored jute, with touches of dull blue and bright crimson. The owner told me that he bought it at an arts-and-crafts shop, but any careful worker could carry out the idea. It was made in double crochet and worked over a filling thread. Later I learned that a strong steel hook, set in a wooden handle, was used. The rug was oblong in shape and was started on a chain of the required width. A simple block pattern was used; the border was formed by crocheting two chains and then a double crochet as the work progressed. Fringe finished the rug, and that was made by cutting pieces of jute ten inches long and tying them into the work on the wrong side.

Round rugs can also be crocheted from jute. These are made by chaining three and forming a ring, into which eight single crochets are worked. The work continues in single crochets, widening and shaping as the rug progresses.

An oval jute rug is started with a chain of forty stitches. It is widened as the work progresses in order that it may not hoop. As is the case with other well-made jute rugs, the ends of the rows are woven through the preceding stitches. As the work changes from one color to another, the loose ends are pulled through as described, and the new color is started in a different place.

X

PATCHWORK AND BUTTON RUGS

I THINK there is no doubt that from the standpoint of real antiquity the patchwork rug is one of the oldest types known. From a very early period in Egyptian history, floor and seat coverings made of linen, interwoven with colored threads, were used in the temples and in the palaces of the Pharaohs. We know that patchwork was a form of needlework known to the Egyptians as early as 900 B.C. The canopy of the bier of an early Egyptian queen, displaying this kind of handiwork, is preserved in the museum at Cairo. All this leads up to the fact that a marble slab, evidently a copy of an Assyrian floor covering, is said by experts to portray a lotus design in patchwork.

Patchwork was made from the earliest days of American colonization, and the art was part of every girl's education. I hope that you are familiar with *A New England Girlhood*, by Lucy Larcom. In it she says, "We learned to make patchwork at school, while we were learning the alphabet; and almost every girl, large or small, had a bedquilt of her own begun with an eye to future home-furnishing."

We may well believe that so universal an art was applied by Colonial dames and maids not only to bedquilt, cushion, and stool cover, but also to the indispensable rug.

I have a friend who proudly displays upon the walls of his hall two cherished patchwork rugs. They are made of antique woolen materials, similar to flannel and colored with ancient vegetable dyes. The backgrounds of both rugs are black and are ornamented with appliquéd designs of trailing vines and flowers. The edges are finished with scallops of the background material, and the rugs are lined throughout. They give a quaint and picturesque touch to the hall.

Right here I must tell you of a cushion which this same man discovered at the time he found the rugs. Two circles, each twenty-two inches in diameter, were cut from flannel. Exactly in the centre of one piece was placed a four-inch circle cut from orange-colored cloth. This circle was buttonhole-stitched to the black background. A dignified cat, evidently with irreproachable manners, was cut from the black cloth and appliquéd on the orange circle. His eyes and nose were embroidered in white floss, his mouth was red, and his stiff whiskers black. Around the orange circle and at equal distances were arranged three orange-colored leaves and three green leaves. The colors were placed alternately. Clover leaves cut from orange cloth were placed between the points of the leaves, and their stems were embroidered in outline stitch with heavy blue floss. Six two-inch hearts made from yellow flannel and six of the same size made of lavender flannel were

Owned by Mrs. Charles Corey

PATCHWORK RUG MADE FROM THE CLOTHING WORN IN THE NORTHERN ARMY DURING THE CIVIL WAR
BY THE OWNER'S GRANDFATHER

arranged at equal distances above the leaves, and a ring of green flannel, one and one half inches wide, was appliquéd around the outside edge of the foundation. The cover was completed by a row of black cloth scallops.

But this is wandering away from rugs. I am describing this cushion cover just to show you some ideas of old-fashioned workers with patchwork! To the eye of the up-to-date housewife, the rugs described above would seem most impractical for use upon the floor; but the same idea, carried out in heavier, more durable materials, might give an exceedingly decorative effect. In fact, appliquéd rugs are now being made by promoters of applied hand industries, and the ideas are worthy of being copied by the woman who wishes pretty things for her home.

I have found that felt is the best material to use in making patchwork rugs. You can buy it from firms dealing in handicraft supplies, or you can purchase a heavy undyed felting from paper mills at a certain price per pound. This can be colored any desired shade.

As with hooked rugs, a number of shapes are found in these rugs made of felt. Ovals are often seen; the rectangular shape is perhaps the most simple to make; the half-rug or door rug serves its purpose just as well when made of patchwork as when it is drawn in.

Simple patterns are the best to use. Baskets of flowers or fruit, similar to the designs appliquéd on cloth, and semiconventional wreaths of flowers and rosettes are easy to work out. If you make your own patterns, you must draw two exactly alike. One is to transfer upon the foundation material, the other is to use in cutting out the appliquéd pieces. Heavy brown paper or light cardboard is good material to use for the patterns.

Now you are ready for the actual work. After you have cut out the shape of the rug, draw the pattern upon it. Then cut out the pieces to be appliquéd. Felt does not fray, so you will not need to allow for turning in the edges. Baste the entire design upon the background before attempting to do the appliqué work. Interesting borders to complete the design are made of strips of the felting. You will find it necessary on oval, round, and half-rugs to cut rounding borders and oftentimes to piece them.

The best thread to use for sewing is gray or natural-colored carpet warp. Buttonhole stitch is used and great care must be taken to keep the stitches even. After the embroidery is finished, press the rug on the wrong side with a damp cloth and a hot iron. Complete the work by lining with denim or burlap. Cut the lining an inch wider than the rug. Turn the denim back on the wrong side and hem close to the edge.

Chenille rugs are first cousins to patchwork rugs,

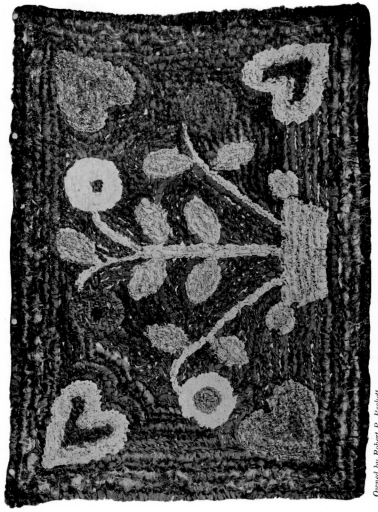

OLD CHENILLE RUG, NOW USED AS A WALL DECORATION

and for that reason should be listed with them. They are made of home-manufactured braid, applied in patterns upon a foundation. Half-inch bias strips of woolen cloth are cut and sewed together. The strips are gathered closely through the centre, using a thread which will not break from the pulling necessary to bring the gathering into place. This gathered strip is then rolled between the palms of the hands until it is formed into a kind of braid. Any kind of cloth of firm texture may be used for the background, and a rough design may be marked upon it to gauge your pattern. You will find that large, simple patterns are the most satisfactory for this type of rug, and if you are an amateur, you had best sew upon your background alternate rows of pleasing colors, finished with a black border, for sewing the chenille braid upon the background requires some ingenuity. After the braid is applied, it is clipped in order that the rug may have a uniform surface.

If you are one of the persons who can remember back to the days when the tin peddler drove his cart, with its shining array of tin dishes, glass hand-lamps, and odds and ends, up to your grandmother's door, you know the period when button rugs came into being. I feel certain that these were invented by some economical woman who wished to use up scraps of cloth too small for braiding and too heavy for drawing in. They were made by appliquéing "buttons" made of three circles of cloth upon a foundation of heavy material. The rugs were cut in different shapes. My grandmother had two octagonal button rugs which ornamented the floor of the shuttered parlor. One of them was placed before a mantel upon which were arranged two delicate vases of Bristol glass, filled with dried feather grass and life everlasting, a Majolica vase containing three peacock feathers, two small spark lamps of Sandwich glass, and a nondescript statuette of a child and a lamb. Grandmother evidently had an eye for harmony; both of those rugs were carefully carried out in shades of brown, tan, and fawn.

A very beautiful button rug belongs to an elderly woman in Franconia, New Hampshire. It is oblong in shape, and delicate colors with blue predominating are used for the buttons. The colors are arranged to form a pattern of large diamonds, and the ends of the rug are finished with a handsome fringe of gray yarn.

Button rugs are very pretty for bedroom use, as the color scheme may be carried out to match hangings. Unfortunately, they will not stand so much hard usage as braided and hooked rugs; but in a room where there is not too much wear and tear they are most suitable. No special outfit is required for the work, and it can be carried about in a bag as easily as a bit of embroidery. It is astonishing how quickly such a rug will grow if the buttons are made at odd minutes.

BUTTON RUG

First, let's talk about materials. Velvet and silk can be used, but are not the best, by any means. Flannels are suitable; most satisfactory of all are pieces of broadcloth and light felt. Almost any firm piece of cloth will do for the foundation.

There are two methods of making the buttons, but these are alike in one thing: three circles of cloth are needed, varying in diameter, one inch for the top circle, one and one half inches for the next circle, and two inches for the undermost circle. By the first method of making the buttons, the edges of all the circles are buttonhole-stitched in colored floss and they are fastened together, one upon the other, by means of French knots through the centre. I prefer the second method, because the rugs are more compact and do not catch the dust so easily: One circle is placed upon the other — the smallest on top, of course — and the edges of each circle are buttonhole-stitched to the one beneath it.

This is the way that the buttons are arranged on the foundation: A button is sewed exactly upon the centre of the background. If the first method of making buttons is used, French knots hold it in place; if the second method is used, the outer circle is buttonhole-stitched to the foundation. A row of buttons is arranged around the centre; then another row; and so on until the rug is finished. You can use various methods in the arrangement of colors, but an effective rug is made by having diagonal stripes of the same color run to the corners. One very lovely rug has the top circles of all the buttons made of black cloth. Another rug is oblong in shape; it has a green denim foundation; the buttons are of shades of brown and tan, with all the top circles made of orange felt. This rug was made in a manner slightly different from the rest — the buttons stood side by side in rows, and the first row was started at one end instead of in the centre.

You should allow enough cloth on the foundation to hem back for a finish. If you wish an especially durable rug, line with unbleached muslin.

A woman in Laconia, New Hampshire, has shown me a "fish-scale" rug which she brought from Nova Scotia. It is a variation of the button idea, being made upon a foundation and constructed from waste bits of cloth. Half-ovals of woolen cloth are button-hole-stitched about the edges with varicolored threads. Three of these half-ovals, varying in size, are used to form one scale. In this rug all of the lower half-ovals were black. The pieces of cloth forming a scale are sewed together on the straight edges, leaving the curving portions free. A row of scales is then arranged along the short side of the rectangular foundation. Then comes another row, overlapping the first row about an inch. This method of arrangement is continued until the foundation is covered.

XI

CROSS–STITCH RUGS

THE cross-stitch rug is an outgrowth of a form of needlework which was popular as far back in history as the Middle Ages. In 1640 was published the twelfth edition of *The Praise of the Needle*, a poem by John Taylor. In these quaint stanzas are references to various stitches used in needlework by the women of the time: —

Fine Ferne-stitch, Finny-stitch, New Stitch, and Chain-stitch,
Brave Bred-stitch, Fisher-stitch, Irish-stitch, and Queen stitch,
The Spanish-stitch, Rosemary-stitch, and Mouse-stitch,
The smarting Whip-stitch, Back-stitch, and the Crosse-stitch,
All these are good, and these we must allow,
And these are everywhere in practice now.

So you see, crosse-stitch, as Taylor called it, was worked upon coarse-meshed fabrics in 1640. Later, after the sampler had developed from the crude records of needlework stitches used by the ladies of the court of Catherine of Aragon to pictures of houses, public buildings, Biblical scenes, and mourning tokens, embellished with borders of leaves, flowers, alphabets, and numerals, and bearing the names of the workers, cross-stitch became a common and popular form of needlecraft. It was used to decorate pillow tops, stool covers, and chair cushions. It continued to develop in popularity through the Victorian period, and there are evidences that certain types of cross-stitch rugs were made in those times. To-day it is used upon household linens, wearing apparel, and bags, and for all kinds of decoration in homes, including artistic rugs. Even the sampler has come again into favor, and modern craftswomen are designing samplers with as much enthusiasm as did their ancestors of the Revolutionary period.

Many articles decorated with cross-stitch are made upon canvas or other coarse, even-meshed fabrics, so the background of the cross-stitch rug must be similar in texture. Well-made burlap, similar to that used in hooked rugs, is good for the foundation material, or a very large-meshed canvas may be used. It should be cut to the desired size, and in all cases should be cut upon a thread. You should have a set of frames to hold the canvas or burlap, for, though you do not need so elaborate a set as for making a hooked rug, yet it must be true and firm in construction. You can make the frames yourself from four straight strips of wood, fastened firmly at the corners. The foundation material should be turned back an inch on all edges, and it should be fastened to the frames by means of thumb tacks. Do not commence your work near the edges of the frames, but leave at least an inch and one half of unworked canvas about the entire rug. These rugs may be made in all shapes — rectangular, oval, round, hexagonal, or octagonal. Whatever shape you decide to make, follow the directions given under hooked rugs.

For filling materials you will need very heavy knitting worsted or the jute described in the chapter on crocheted rugs. You can use up odds and ends of worsteds by pulling from three to four strands of it through the eyes of the needle. The needle should have a large eye and a blunt point, that it may not catch in the meshes of the canvas. Tapestry needles are excellent for this work.

Nearly every needleworker knows how to do cross-stitch, but for the benefit of anyone to whom it is a new art, I will give a brief description. I have spoken before of *A Hand-Book of Needlework*, written eighty-odd years ago by Miss Lambert. It is interesting alike to the collector of old books and to the needleworker.

The book-collector will find great interest in the preface, in which the author quaintly says: "I am indebted to my husband for his assistance in some of the historical notices, and again for his permission in allowing my maiden name to appear on the title-page, as being that by which I am more generally recognized in my avocation." The needleworker will discover that Miss Lambert's descriptions of old stitches are as good as the day they were written. Let me quote her description of doing cross-stitch: —

"Cross-stitch is worked over two threads in a diagonal direction each way. It is a double stitch, and made, first by bringing the needle up on the left and putting it down on the right, which forms half a stitch; it is then crossed by bringing the needle up again on the right and passing it down on the left. We would advise each stitch to be finished before another is commenced, as the work will be more even than if it were half stitched before crossing — a

Courtesy of "The Country Gentleman"

THIS PICTURE SHOWS THE METHOD OF WORKING THE CROSS-STITCH RUG

method not infrequently practised. Grounding in cross-stitch should be done in alternate rows backwards and forwards."

Points for you to remember, when making a cross-stitch rug, are to cross your stitches all the same way and, if you have used canvas instead of burlap, to take up from two to four small squares instead of one.

Now comes the selection of the design. Look over your cross-stitch patterns and select one with clear-cut, bold outlines, remembering, as you do so, that the design will be greatly enlarged when it is completed. If you wish to make your own designs, buy the checked paper used by artists and designers, and draw your patterns by the aid of the small blocks upon the paper.

Conventional and geometrical patterns are easy to do, and simple block patterns will use up the odds and ends of yarn which collect in every household. Squares, rectangles, and diamonds may be easily worked out with varicolored wools, divided off with black wools.

Picture rugs, similar to those made upon hooked rugs, can be made, if the picture selected is not too intricate. Samplers will furnish ideas for them. Figures of children are especially pretty upon rugs for children's rooms and nurseries. Animal designs may be made in cross-stitch. Children are always fond of any kind of rug bearing pictures of lambs, kittens, dogs, ducks, and chickens.

If you choose a floral pattern, keep it simple. Large single roses, fleur-de-lis — in fact, any broad-petaled flowers may be used either in a border or for a central motif. In all cases follow your pattern very closely, or you will lose the shape of the design. A border of leaves is effective.

The question of color is as important in these as in any other kind of handmade rugs. Neutral or subdued colors — tans, grays, dull blues, soft browns, black, and ivory — make excellent backgrounds, and in rugs where the design is simple, vivid coloring may be introduced with good effect.

The work on a cross-stitch rug goes very quickly, and almost before you know it your rug is completed. To finish it, take it from the frames, fold back the canvas at the outermost line of the cross-stitching, and press it on the back with a hot iron. It adds to the beauty of the work if the entire rug is pressed before lining. Then line it with felting, flannel, denim, or heavy cotton cloth. In the case of rugs other than those of rectangular or square shapes, follow the directions given for finishing hooked rugs.

Some of the older cross-stitch rugs introduced raised flowers in certain sections of the design. Loops of wool were pulled through the canvas in a manner similar to that of hooking in. After the design was all pulled in with shaded wools, the pattern was clipped with sharp scissors until the form of the desired design appeared upon the surface, above the rest of the rug. The result was similar to the embossed surfaces of hooked rugs where the designs were raised above the backgrounds.

Miss Lambert in her old book on needlework tells

CROSS-STITCH RUG IN RED AND BLACK

of this method of raised cut-embroidery in wool. As I told you, the book was first published in England. In a certain part she refers briefly to a rug which I feel sure was similar to the American hooked rug. While describing the raised embroidery, she refers to a so-called "mesh" for pulling the wool through the cloth. The description and the drawing of the implement suggest to me the rug hook. Later she says: "This description of work is best adapted to succeed on cloth; if properly done, it should be extremely firm and solid, so that, if trodden upon, it will be but little injured." Then she continues farther on: "The method we have described will be found the best, where perfection of raised work is sought for; but a more simple mode of working is over a common wooden mesh, and cutting with the scissors, in a similar manner to the raised edges of urn rugs."

Just what urn rugs were, I do not know, but I think there is no doubt but they were related to the rug made of a combination of cross-stitch and raised cut-embroidery in wool, and to the hooked rug. The author of the quaint book tells us that "raised work of this kind has been brought to great perfection, particularly in France, both for flowers, birds, and animals." Shall we look then to the French crafts workers of the past for the models of certain types of our New England rugs?

XII

ODDS AND ENDS

My grandmother's kitchen was a cheerful place. It was the centre of the household — the factory where the many industries necessary to home life on a large farm were carried on. The old fireplace was closed, but on Thanksgiving Grandmother carried out the old customs and once more built a fire in the huge brick oven. Then the coals were raked back, and dozens of pies were baked. The mince and apple pies, by the way, were carried out into the cold "buttery" and frozen for winter consumption.

The homestead had belonged to the family for a number of generations, and the mellow charm of used things hung about it. I remember sitting in my little straight-backed rocking-chair, clutching to me Whitenose, the big black-and-white family cat, and watching Grandmother as she bustled about the kitchen. Then, after the dinner dishes were done and she had arrayed herself in a snowy, crackling, starched apron, she would tell Minnie, the "hired girl," to bring a basket of corn husks from the corn chamber. Grandmother had saved the soft inner husks from husking time, and she used them to make rugs.

Yes, rugs! Corn-husk rugs were made by the early colonists, an old parchment-bound account book tells us. In it we read that some woman of the past paid for "1 Gaus handkerchief" with "1 bushel of nuts and a corn-husk rug." Those Grandmother made were used before the outside kitchen door, in the entry and on the porch, to keep the tracks of muddy shoes off the white-scrubbed kitchen floor. You will find them excellent for porch use. The method of making the braids followed that of plaiting braided rugs, although there were some variations in the work. Grandmother tied six of the white husks together and fastened them with a bit of twine halfway down their length. She divided these into three parts, each part containing two husks. Then she began to braid, but as she brought the "three" strand into place she added two new husks. The secret of the process lay in wrapping the short ends of a strand in the new husks. When Grandmother had a braid of sufficient length to make a round rug, she fastened the end firmly with twine. Dry corn husks are too brittle to sew together, so she placed the braid in water and let it stand overnight. The next morning she drained off the water. By afternoon the braid was in exactly the right condition for working, and the rug was sewn together by the same method as that described for making round braided rugs.

But I was not always an onlooker at these tasks. In good old New Hampshire style, Grandmother believed that Satan finds mischief for idle hands to do! So she taught me to make a simple rug by stringing small bits of woolen cloth on a piece of twine, by means of a darning needle. These pieces of cloth were about two inches long and an inch wide and were of all colors of the rainbow. Each cloth necklace was about a yard long, and Grandmother sewed them later on a background of heavy print, three quarters of a yard wide and a yard long. The rugs were soft and warm, though unfortunately they caught every bit of dust. Nevertheless, they served their purpose in providing occupation for small hands.

Once I was visiting another child whose mother, no doubt, found us too active for her comfort, so she set us to making rugs, from an idea that she had learned in Canada in her own childhood. Upon unbleached muslin she drew a swan, supposed to be swimming on an azure lake. Our work was to ruffle narrow lengths of thin cloth and to sew them on the design, taking our stitches through the ruffling stitches. I shall never forget it! The swan developed without much effort on our part, but the work of "ruffling" sky and water seemed endless, and when we reached the black border we had to be coaxed and threatened into finishing our rug.

The only rug that — for want of a better name — I must call a star rug, I saw many years ago in the little village of Gilmanton Iron Works, New Hampshire. Cousin Charles was the village postmaster, and he and Cousin Abbie lived to be very old, but their house, filled with things that would have made an antique-collector's mouth water, was burned in a fire that swept through the unprotected village. I remember the rug, because Abbie May's wax doll, in a blue "polonaise," sat solemnly in her chair which was placed upon it. I have only recently worked out from an old-fashioned cushion cover the idea of the manufacture of that rug, but I feel certain that any modern craftswoman can make one.

Velvet squares formed the background of Cousin Abbie's rug, but squares of broadcloth would serve the purpose just as well. In working out my pattern from the pillow cover, I decided that nine-inch squares would be the best size to use.

Now let me tell you exactly how to make the stars. A five-pointed star of cardboard, tin, or zinc is fastened to the centre of a square and a darning needle is threaded with doubled four-ply Germantown. Commencing with the tip of one point, the yarn is pulled through the fabric, over and over the cardboard foundation, until all five points are covered. The sewing must be done as closely and thickly as possible, to ensure a velvety appearance when the star is done. In covering the pattern, the centre is left open. Starting from this centre and using a pair of sharp scissors, cut each point straight through to the tip. Carefully remove the stiff pattern through the opening in the worsted, and a fluffy star made of Germantown will remain. You can make the stars all of one color, using varied colors in the points, or obtain a mottled effect by introducing odds and ends of worsteds into the star. Featherstitch the squares together, and complete with a border of silken braids. (Here's a suggestion for using old silk stockings.) Line the rug with any kind of firm cloth.

I am sure that you have seen rugs made from pieces of "boughten" carpets and finished with braided strips. From a collector's standpoint they are worthless, but they are extremely useful in summer cottages. The prettiest one that I have seen was made from a small triangle of blue carpeting, bordered by gray-and-blue braids. It was used in a blue-and-white bedroom that overlooked the sea.

Another rug — which reminds me forcibly of the Pueblo Indian sleeping mat, not in materials used but in the construction — is made of strips of felt, each about one half inch wide. A simple frame of the desired size is constructed of slats of wood, and the rug is woven in the same manner as the paper mats made by kindergarten children. One color is used for the strips of the warp and a contrasting and harmonizing shade is used for the woof. The places where the warp and woof intermingle, at the sides and the ends of the rug, are fastened with heavy threads, and the ends of the pieces of felt are left loose for a finish.

There are certain by-products of rug-making which furnish ideas for craftswomen interested in constructing simple articles of beauty and utility.

The first stools with hooked tops that I saw were in the White Cupboard Inn at Woodstock, Vermont. They were designed by Mrs. Elizabeth Royce, and were quaint and artistic.

There are different ways of obtaining the wooden stools. You may have them built at your cabinet-maker's, or you may find just the one for which you are looking in a secondhand furniture store or an antique shop. The owner of an old homestead on the Oxbow in Newbury, Vermont, discovered two stools tucked away under the eaves in her attic. Either three- or four-legged stools are used. I think that you will find it necessary to paint such a stool, and you can use either black, gray, or ivory enamel to match the room in which you are to use it.

For the hooked top use as a foundation a piece of fine-meshed burlap. The shape may be circular, oval, square, or rectangular, depending upon the top of the stool. Allow at least two extra inches for finishing. Make a frame of four slats of light wood and sew the stool top into it. Mark a simple pattern of a wreath of old-fashioned posies, a basket of flowers, or any simple spray of flowers. Landscape designs may be used, if they are kept very simple indeed. Cross-stitch patterns can be readily adapted to these hooked tops, and a careful study of them will repay the designer. Knitting worsteds are the best materials for hooking in, but scraps of silk and satins may be used. The method of working is exactly the same as that of making hooked rugs.

After the hooking is completed, remove the stool
top from the frames, leaving the border for turning
in. Pad the top of the stool with layers of outing
flannel or half-worn blankets. Arrange the hooked
top over the padding, and fasten in place with up-
holstery tacks. Complete the edge by carefully tacking on a fringe made of knitting worsteds in black or
neutral colors.

Some of the arts-and-crafts shops are displaying
hooked collar-and-cuff sets. They are especially effective when used on flannel or jersey-cloth dresses.
Curtain scrim is used for the foundation material
and is held in place in ordinary embroidery frames.
Knitting worsteds are used for filling in, and the hooking is done with a medium-sized steel crochet hook.
Very simple patterns are used, and frequently the collar
and cuffs have borders matching the gown in color.

Scrim is also used for the foundation of hooked
bags. The cloth is cut in a rectangle large enough to
fold to make a bag of the required size. It is held in
place in embroidery hoops. Worsteds or strips of
fine silk are used for the work. As in the case of
the stool tops and the collar-and-cuff sets, simple
patterns are best.

The art of hooking in is now being applied to the
decoration of gowns. Jersey cloth is the best material,
and simple patterns and borders of plain stripes of
color make the decoration. One dress was made of
tan jersey, and had about the bottom a three-inch

Courtesy of Mrs. E. E. Morse and "The House Beautiful"

THESE STOOLS WITH HOOKED TOPS WILL FURNISH IDEAS FOR CRAFTS-
WOMEN INTERESTED IN CONSTRUCTING SIMPLE ARTICLES
OF BEAUTY AND UTILITY

brown and orange band, pulled in with doubled strands of Iceland wool. Dark blue jersey cloth with a border of gray and royal blue is another suggestion.

In a novelty shop, not long ago, I saw some porch and lawn seats, designed, the shopkeeper told me, by a farm woman. They were made of fine rag braids in the same way that round braided rugs are made, and were just the size of grass lawn-mats. Handles for carrying them were formed of loops of the braids sewed into shape. These seats were gay indeed — red, yellow, orange, and bright blue predominating in them. They were very salable and the designer was frequently asked to refill orders.

I have also seen bags made of braided silk pieces. Two round mats of the desired sizes are constructed. They are sewed together with an opening left at the top, and a braided handle is made and attached to the top of the bag.

Patchwork pictures are interesting to design and are lovely for decorations. Coarse-woven linens and unbleached muslin make excellent backgrounds, and bright bits of cloth from the piece bag will furnish the patches. If you have any imagination at all, you will enjoy creating landscapes, seascapes, garden scenes, and quaint big-hooped maidens, hidden coyly under poke bonnets. The appliqué work is done with small stitches in colored threads to match the materials, and sometimes it will be necessary to add a bit of embroidery to get just the desired effect.

XIII

THE WOVEN RUG

It is not because I think the art of making the woven rug less important than the construction of other kinds that I have left its discussion until this chapter. It is rather because the subject is so extensive that it would be impossible to write fully upon it in a book on general rug-making. We might almost say it needs a book by itself, but, on the other hand, one could not write of handmade New England rugs without speaking of this form of old-time handicraft.

Weaving and spinning are as old as written history, and as universal as mankind. All primitive tribes have had their crude forms of these crafts. The Book of Proverbs tells of that woman whose price was far above rubies: "She seeketh wool and flax, and worketh willingly with her hands. . . . She layeth her hands to the spindle, and her hands hold the distaff."

Roman matrons, even ladies of royal status, prided themselves upon their knowledge of the loom, and supervising the weaving in large households was part of their daily duty.

Early New England women brought the knowledge with them to the forest-covered lands of their new home. As time went on and farms were cleared, the daughters on all the isolated farms learned to weave, that they might assist in replenishing the stock of household linens and add, bit by bit, to the necessary articles for their own setting-out. Sometimes they were aided by the professional weaver, who traveled about to help them prepare the warps and assist them in threading looms.

There are women still living who can remember when weaving and spinning were New England home industries. The flax field, with its crown of fragile blue flowers, was a necessary part of every farm, and the failure of the crop was thought a great misfortune. Every farmer owned a flock of sheep.

Can't you picture the women of the family, seated out of doors on summer afternoons, drawing from their little flax wheels the threads to be woven on the big loom? And there was constantly the whir of the big spinning wheels, for we are told that it required the work of four spinners to supply one loom.

In her book, *New England Bygones*, Mrs. Rollins gives us a charming picture of weaving as she recalled it: "My grandmother used to sit, hour after hour, at her loom, plying the shuttle with no less persistence than in spinning she drew out her threads. Across the huge beams (of the loom), under and over each other crossed and recrossed these threads, like a spider's web. The work was slow, but it never flagged. Threads were broken and carefully taken up; quills gave out, and were patiently renewed; the web grew, thread by thread, inch by inch; the intricate pattern came out upon the surface and pleased the weaver's eye. . . . At the end of a long summer's afternoon the end of the warp was reached; the treadles slipped; the web was done."

It is not strange that our grandmothers early called upon an art which they knew so well to furnish them with coverings for their floors. Handwoven rag carpets were used in many New England farmhouses and village homes. A friend of mine inherited a small house in a little New Hampshire village. When she came to examine her inheritance she found that every floor in the house, except those of the kitchen and the buttery, was covered with hand-woven rag carpeting! It was the work of an elderly woman who had inherited a cumbersome old-time loom from her mother. As a child, she had helped her mother weave carpets for the village housewives and, to use her own phraseology, had woven carpeting enough in her life "to nearly go round the world." It is perhaps worthy of note that this weaver, now nearly eighty years old, is still earning her living by making rugs on the ancient loom.

Modern craftswomen who have revived the arts of their grandmothers are weaving rugs for their own use and for commercial purposes. No one can weave well without a good loom adapted for the kind of weaving preferred by the worker. Ancient Colonial looms can sometimes be put in good working order, but even the largest modern looms are less cumber-

Courtesy of Mary Meigs Atwater

MODERN CRAFTSWOMEN WHO HAVE REVIVED THE ART OF THEIR GRAND-
MOTHERS ARE WEAVING RUGS FOR THEIR OWN USE AND FOR
COMMERCIAL PURPOSES

some and take up less space than the old type.
Reduced to its simplest terms, a loom is simply a
framework for stretching the warp and for dividing
the warp into parts for the insertion of the weft —
sometimes called woof or filling. There are various
kinds, from the simple wooden frames which are
hardly more than toys to the clumsy machines of
the past. In Colonial days looms set up with
harness of two heddle frames were used for the
weaving of plain linen sheets, linsey-woolsey, or
plain rag carpeting.

The process of stringing up the loom was as follows: Usually two women worked together, one
holding the warp threads while the other turned the
crank for winding the warp on the warp beam at
the back of the loom. The harness of two heddle
frames hung from the overstructure. The threading
was carried through the heddle eyes alternately,
first in the front frame, then in the back frame.
Then the batten was threaded, and the warp was
passed over the breastbeam and secured to the cloth
beam.

When the foot of the worker was pressed on the
treadle tied to the first heddle frame, that frame was
depressed and the second was raised. This made
what was called a "shed." Through this shed, between the warp threads, the worker passed the shuttle, filled with the weft thread. Then she pushed
the weft into place by means of the batten. Using

the other treadle, and the over and under interlacing of threads, she repeated the process.

Two-harness looms are in use to-day, but they cannot serve for pattern weaving. The best apparatus to select is a large treadle loom equipped with four harnesses and weaving forty-four inches wide. It can be used for both plain and pattern weaving.

Mary Meigs Atwater, an authority on weaving, does not find the plain rag rugs of the hit-or-miss variety interesting. She suggests copying the patterns of the old-fashioned coverlets, and constructing a rug design of character. A study of these old coverlets will more than repay the craftswoman who takes pleasure in creative work.

The warp thread used in weaving rugs is strong and durable; it comes in black, natural, or gray, and is now made in other colors. It can be purchased from various department stores, from some arts-and-crafts shops, from professional weavers, and from the large mail-order houses.

Almost any kind of cloth can be used for the weft of the old-style rag rugs. Old clothing and household linens are excellent, and either cotton or woolen cloth may be woven. It is best, however, to keep cotton goods for one rug and woolen for another. One thrifty woman who makes many rugs for herself and her friends tears her worn-out garments, old sheets, and other household linens into strips of the required size and puts them away in paper bags. Then, when she has enough for a rug, she brings them out and dyes them. For pattern weaving, cotton "roving," jute rug-filling, woolen rug-yarn, and cotton chenille are excellent materials.

There is a certain knack in sewing carpet rags. The cloth should be cut or torn into strips varying in size with the thickness of the material. Three quarters of an inch is a desirable width for goods of the quality of gingham. The method of sewing is as follows: Place the end of one rag by the end of the other and fold the strips lengthwise for about two inches. Then make two firm stitches through the center of the sides of the fold. This is done that there may be no bunches in the woven rug. Then break the thread. After some practice you will be able to sew quickly. Wind your rags in balls — one color to a ball, unless you are making hit-or-miss carpeting. Some rug-weavers claim that one pound of carpet rags makes a yard of carpeting, so if you wish to plan your material, you might weigh the rags and wind into balls containing one half pound each.

The color question is important in weaving rugs. The study of the shades in antique coverlets will give inspiration, and there are more modern combinations which are exquisite. A very pretty hit-or-miss rug, used in a dining-room, was woven from woolen scraps in shades of gray, blue, dull green, and orange, with black scraps scattered frequently among them. It was made upon gray warp, and a border of blue-

and-black was added at each end. Three strips of carpeting were sewn together to make the rug.

It would be difficult to give in this short chapter explicit directions for weaving a rug upon the large four-harness loom, and it would be misleading to give directions for weaving one upon a table loom, as that type is too small for rug-weaving. Beginners, however, find it much easier to learn to weave on a small loom before progressing to the larger size. Merely to offer a suggestion, and to give the crafts-woman an idea of the simple process of weaving, that she may receive an incentive to become inter-ested in a worth-while creative handicraft, the proc-ess of weaving a table runner of silk pieces will be described.

First, let me attempt to give some general direc-tions for weaving. The first thing is to thread the loom. Decide upon the length of your runner, then add eighteen inches extra to the length of each warp thread. Now determine how many warp threads cover one inch, and multiply that by the width of the runner, allowing one half inch extra for the sel-vage. If you look at the cross frame, you will see that it contains a series of small holes with regular spaces between them. Thread the warp threads al-ternately in the holes and across the spaces. Choose a thread for the right side of the runner, and pull it through a slot at the proper distance from the centre. Continue this process, alternately filling the holes

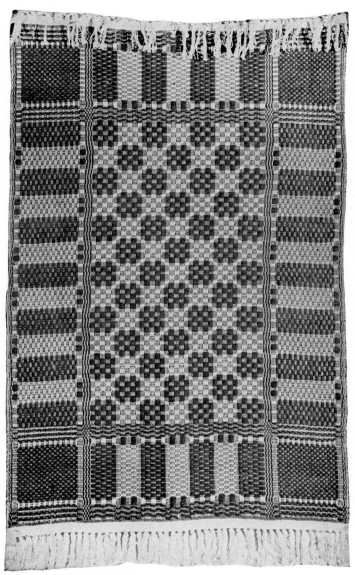

WOVEN RUG. "DOG-TRACKS" PATTERN

and spaces. Loop the ends in front of the frame to keep the threads from slipping for the time being. Now lock the back roller of the loom, and knot the ends of the warp thread into groups. Pull one of the two matched sticks which come with the table loom through the tab on the back roller; then through half of the loops of the knotted threads; then through the centre tab; then through the other half of the knotted warp threads; then through the remaining tabs. Hold the warp threads in the right hand as tightly as possible, and, having unlocked the back roller, turn it away from you, and roll the threads evenly upon it. When about a foot of the warp threads remains, lock the roller, and loop the ends of the warp threads until you are ready to slip the other matched stick through the tabs, and warp and wind it on the front roller.

The runner that I am describing is made of sand-colored strips, and the border is old blue, rose, and dull green on a natural-colored warp. Wind the silk strips on the shuttle. Lift the cross frame and bring it forward until it is within a short distance of the back roller. Pass the shuttle through this opening. Drop the cross frame and bring it forward. You must use both hands, and press the weft of silk rags as far forward as it will go. Now push the cross frame back near the back roller, but do not lift it; instead, force it down. Pass the shuttle through this opening; bring the cross frame forward, and press the new weft against the first filling of weft. Continue this process, and you will find your web beginning to grow. After a number of inches have been woven, the web must be rolled upon the front roller and more of the unwoven warp then brought forward. First weave three inches of the sand-colored material, then six rows of old blue, two rows of rose, six rows of blue, five of rose, one of green, and four of blue. Then weave with the sand color until you have the desired length. Now add the other border, reversing it as you work. To remove the work from the loom, cut the warp threads in front of the cross frame, loosen the roller, and unwind the material. To finish the runner, stitch the ends upon the sewing machine, and tie the warp to form fringe.

After you have once mastered the simple rudiments of weaving, the process is not difficult, and the purchase of a large four-harness treadle-loom will enable you to weave rugs with patterns or plain rugs with intricate borders. It is an understood thing that this type of loom is threaded not for one rug, but to make a web of carpeting, or a number of rugs, with the same threading. Directions come with the different types of looms; but it would be wise for the beginner to get in touch with a professional weaver and take a few lessons in rug-weaving.

XIV

EMBROIDERED CARPETS

ALTHOUGH embroidered carpets were produced by a few ambitious American craftswomen during the early years of the nineteenth century, the amount of work required for their execution made them the exception rather than the rule in the realm of needlework. At a time when a woman had to superintend, at least, all the sewing of clothes for the members of her family and of the linens for her household, she could hardly undertake the task of embroidering a floor covering which would take all her spare time for two to nine years or so. She might attempt a chair back, a table cover, an ottoman, a fire screen, or, in the forties, a piece of the popular Berlin work which had superseded the sampler stampede of Revolutionary days, but the making of a carpet required hours of leisure that a woman of the early republic did not usually have. Women whose husbands were beginning to make money in the new era of commercial activity were buying French and English factory-made carpets of floral design, which were being steadily distributed throughout the United States. Embroidered carpets may have been the outgrowth of the desires of less affluent women, who were hungering for beauty in their homes, and who felt that they were taking one step in the right direction when they made coverings for their parlor floors.

These handmade carpets were not of American origin, nor were they characteristic of the nineteenth century, for they had been made on the Continent and in provincial England for many generations. We hear of them in Germany as early as the fifteenth century — the forerunners, no doubt, of the unique needle-point rugs made by German women in Pennsylvania. One Pennsylvania German embroidered carpet, owned by Mrs. J. Insley Blair, is worked in cross-stitch, carrying out a geometric design which is obviously a sampler pattern, and is further adorned by billing doves, which convey the impression that it was originally intended for the parlor of a bride.

Embroidered carpets were commonly enough made in England to warrant reference to them in Miss Lambert's *Hand-Book of Needlework*, of which I have previously spoken. Writing of English lambswool, this craftswoman of the late eighteen-thirties advocates its use combined with German wool, for the making of carpets.

"Worsted is a still harsher description of English wool, manufactured from the coarser parts of the fleece," she wrote; "but it is capable of taking a very fine dye, and may be advantageously used for working carpets and rugs. It is much cheaper than either German or English lambswool, and is the best and only proper material for making the raised borders of urn rugs, and the various kinds of patterns and borders in moss and rouleau, etc.; it being, from the length of its filaments, greatly improved by combing, assuming that downy appearance which distinguishes a well-finished rug border."

Various stitches were used, it seems, in the making of English embroidered carpets, for one attributed to the eighteenth century and owned by the Victoria and Albert Museum is developed in a combination of cross-stitch and chain stitch on canvas.

Because so very few embroidered carpets are left to us for the study of floor coverings in early American homes, the examples which do remain are doubly important as textile evidence. One owned by the Metropolitan Museum of Art is made of burlap strips, worked in cross-stitch and sewed together. The pattern appears to be based on a brocade design and the coloring is uninteresting. It is said to be of New York workmanship, and the surmised date is 1810.

Much more unusual, both in design and workmanship, is the Miner carpet, which gained its name from that of its creator, Mrs. E. G. Miner of Canton, St. Lawrence County, New York. The story is told that Mrs. Miner, after spending her leisure for seven or eight years in making the carpet, completed it in 1844 and sent it to the state fair for exhibition. But the piece of patiently made handicraft arrived too late for the intended purpose, so Mr. Homer Eaton Keyes, the editor of *Antiques*, tells us.

"So much interest did it arouse," Mr. Keyes says,

"that it was given a special display by itself. At the time it was described as showing a border consisting entirely of bouquets of flowers, and a central series picturing groups of cattle, sheep with their shepherds, hunters on the trail of buffalo and moose, game birds, and what not else."

Now the carpet, which was sixteen feet square, has been broken up and the parts distributed among members of the family, precious remembrances of the ancestor who designed and embroidered the ancient floor covering. The designs are naturalistic and were drawn with charcoal upon pieces of bagging, then embroidered, with stocking yarns and ravelings from knitted garments, in what seems to be chain stitch.

All of the traditions of the early craftswomen of rural New England are wrapped up in an embroidered carpet made in the small northern Vermont town of Castleton sometime during the two years or more preceding 1835.[1] Spinning, weaving, home dyeing, patient needlework, and original design contribute to the interest and charm of this example of early nineteenth-century floor covering.

The maker, Zeruah Higley Guernsey, came honestly enough by her knowledge of spinning, for she had grown up in a community where it was necessary for all girls to learn to spin, and, moreover, her

[1] Illustrations of embroidered carpets, including several of the "Caswell Carpet" here reproduced by kind permission of the Editor, appeared in *Antiques*, Vol. IX, No. 6, frontispiece and pp. 396 ff.

father was a maker of spinning wheels. Step by step, from its first stage as unkempt wool upon the sheeps' backs, to the day when the material came from the brass dye-pots ready to be worked upon the home-spun background, the carpet developed under the industrious fingers of its designer. Each square of the carpet — which is twelve feet wide by thirteen and one half feet long — bears a different design. If you look the pattern over ever so carefully, you cannot find two that resemble each other. It reminds the student of early handicrafts of the "Circuit Rider's Quilt," now the valued property of the Chicago Art Institute, which was made for the dauntless Reverend G. C. Warvel by the women of the United Brethren Church at Miami, Ohio. No two squares in the quilt are alike; but there is one great difference between it and the carpet. The quilt was planned by forty different women; the diversity of design in the carpet came from the imagination of but one woman.

The coloring of the wools used in working the carpet is as varied as the designs. Flowers, leaves, ferns, fruits, butterflies, puppies, cats, a rooster, and a man and woman appear in hues which are sometimes true to nature and sometimes flights of fancy. Upon the black background the designs are clearly cut.

I think that it was Bacon who said, "In needle-work and embroideries, it is more pleasing to have a lively work upon a sad and solemn ground than to have a dark and melancholy work upon a lightsome ground." The rather startling blue-and-white cat, the gay flowers, and the bright costumes of the man and woman, etched upon the black background, are practical demonstrations of this theory.

The overornateness of design which was beginning to be noticeable in furniture, in silver and Britannia ware, and in needlework, had evidently not yet permeated to the remote town where Zeruah Higley Guernsey planned the carpet for her father's prim parlor. Although there is a mere touch of massiveness in some of the patterns, most of them follow the open designs and feeling for silhouette prevalent in the eighteenth century.

"Zeruah Guernsey never once loses her feeling for sparkling pattern," says Mr. Keyes, describing this inimitable carpet, "but she does occasionally yield to the dictates of naturalism — not so much in her depiction of the lover and his lass as in that of some tumbling puppies and kittens and of an extraordinary blue cat. In each of the latter three the background is no more than a symbol, devoid of perspective; but it is important, for it unmistakably represents a simple rag carpet. The normal carpeting of Zeruah's house we may therefore safely infer to have been the woven rag strip."

In the actual working out of the patterns the designer seems to have made use of chain stitch, which Miss Lambert defined as an imitation of tambour work. It is said that Zeruah claimed she did the work upon tambour frames, which were formed of two hoops covered with cloth, the material being stretched on the inner, and kept in its place by the outer hoop, tightened by means of a thumbscrew. In 1842, when the American edition of Miss Lambert's book was published, tambour work was evidently out of style, for she wrote, as a definition of the frames, "Tambour frames, whereon the material is stretched like the parchment of a drum — whence their name — are now seldom employed, although formerly much used when tambour work was the fashion." So we can picture Zeruah Guernsey, stretching her squares of black homespun like parchment of a drum upon her frames.

There is an unusual and most interesting addition to this embroidered carpet developed by the designer's desire to conceal the ugliness of the unused parlor hearth in summer time. This hearth piece was detachable, and when it became necessary to build the roaring fires required by rigorous Northern winters in the parlor fireplace, the hearth piece could be removed. We cannot tell why Zeruah lavished her best designs upon this section of the carpet. Was it because she grew up in a period when the huge fireplace formed the centre of family life, or because it seemed to draw attention to a spot of balanced interest to save the best design for the hearth? Whatever the reason, the hearth covering bears a striking pattern of flowers, fruit, and leaves, arranged in a basket, and supplemented on either side by sprays of flowers. On three sides of the unit is a border of red triangles.

In 1846 Zeruah Guernsey married a Caswell, but continued to live in Castleton for many years. As time went on, the famous piece of handiwork which covered the floor of her parlor became known as the Caswell carpet. It is now the property of the editor of *Antiques.*

If old furniture and household possessions could speak and tell us their secrets, what stories we might relate! The Caswell carpet could no doubt entertain us with tales of old New England. There are a few traditions that have come down through the years with it. One is that the blue tabby on the carpet exercised an uncanny influence upon the family house cat when she strayed one day into the parlor. It is said that the insulted pussy arched her back and spit spitefully at the worsted feline.

Three squares of the carpet have unusual interest as autographic data. One bears the initials of the creator, while two others are ornamented with the initials F B and L F M. It is known that F B stood for Francis Baron, and it is thought that L F M represented his companion. These boys were Indians of the Potawatami tribe and were students at the Castleton Medical College. During their medical training these lads were given homes by the village

A SECTION OF THE CASWELL CARPET, NOW OWNED BY MR. HOMER KEYES,
SHOWING A VARIETY OF THE MOST INTERESTING DESIGNS, INCLUDING
THE MAN AND WOMAN WEARING THE COSTUMES OF 1835,
AND THE HEARTH PIECE

people, different families taking their turns. They were guests in the Guernsey family during the period when the carpet was being made, and each contributed a design to it.

Courtesy of "Antiques"

THERE IS A TRADITION THAT THE BLUE TABBY ON THE
CASWELL CARPET EXERCISED AN UNCANNY INFLUENCE
UPON THE FAMILY HOUSE CAT

The man and woman embroidered on the Caswell carpet have had an interesting but rather tedious existence. After the carpet was completed Zeruah covered the unhappy pair with another design tightly sewed over them. They have been freed, however, from their bondage, and now add distinction and historical interest to the work by their clothes, which are costumes of 1835 and verify the date that the Vermont girl embroidered on the edge of the carpet

Courtesy of "Antiques"

SQUARES FROM THE CASWELL CARPET, SHOWING INITIALS AND DATE, WITH THE OPEN DESIGNS AND FEELING FOR SILHOUETTE PREVALENT IN THE EIGHTEENTH CENTURY

which was to bring her name before collectors of early Americana.

Embroidered carpets add an interesting item to the subject of early American floor coverings. The editor of *Antiques* merely suggests that perhaps the embroidered carpet serves as a kind of forerunner of the hooked rug.

"This, rather inevitably, brings us back to the perennial and as yet unanswered question as to the date when hooked rugs first came into use, and as to the nature of the floor coverings which they superseded," he says. "As to the first question, it is provable beyond peradventure that the technique of hooking, almost precisely as it was and is applied in the production of hooked rugs, was known in the eighteenth century; but it was applied to the making of bedcovers, not of carpets. Such bedcovers, wrought in wool yarns on a homespun wool foundation, constitute a chapter yet to be written."

XV

COMMERCIAL OPPORTUNITIES OF
RUG–MAKING

To the woman with creative instinct, artistic sense, and nimble fingers, the rug industry offers an opportunity for supplementing her supply of pin money, or even furnishing means for a livelihood. From a commercial standpoint, hooked, braided, and woven rugs are the most popular, although well-made appliqué rugs of felt, crocheted rugs in artistic colors, knitted rugs, — especially the "washboard" variety, — and button rugs are salable.

There are three ways by which the woman working at home may readily dispose of her wares: she may work and sell her rugs in her own house; she may sell through gift shops and department stores; she may promote a community industry, with herself as the business manager.

The rugs, however, be they hooked, braided, appliquéd, knitted, crocheted, or woven, must be the best products that the worker can make. The designs, while varied, must all be pleasing, the workmanship of the finest type, and the color schemes harmonious. The price must not be too exorbitant. The worker should receive a good price for her work, but she should remember also to be fair to the customer. One dealer — he does not make the rugs, by the way — told me that he preferred to ask less for his wares, in the vernacular "to turn them over more quickly," rather than to keep his money tied up too long. The home worker does not have this question to meet. The one that confronts her is how quickly she wishes to turn her piece of handicraft into ready money. So, first, make a thorough study of your market, carefully estimating each step of your output. Do not expect, at once, to make as large wages as you would if working on a salary outside of your home. The home worker must always remember that she has not the overhead expenses of the outside worker. She is really managing two businesses, those of her home and of her handicraft. Later, as the quality of her wares is perfected and as her reputation grows, she can establish larger prices.

Now, suppose that you are a woman working in your own home; how are you to reach your customers? You can write notes to prospective customers, saying that you have rugs for sale, or you can insert an advertisement in a paper circulating among the people whom you wish to interest in your wares. You can also hang an artistic sign, featuring the rugs, in front of your house; or, if you live in a resort town, you can obtain permission to hang a small poster in hotel offices. Then, as customers come, you can display the rugs which you have at hand and take orders for others. I think that it is advisable to ask more money for a rug made to match certain color schemes, or for one that involves extra work in designing. If you are a countrywoman, an exhibit at state and county fairs may help you.

A simple way of disposing of homemade rugs is to interest the owner of a gift shop, the head of the rug and drapery department of a large store, or an interior decorator. Here you will pay a commission for all rugs sold or for all work ordered.

Perhaps you are one of those persons who has a vision of handicraft work done by a community. One of the best-known instances of such a project is the Society of Deerfield Industries at Deerfield, Massachusetts, where weaving, rug-making, basket-making, ironworking, netting, tufted work, and dyeing, as well as photography, are done by individuals who have banded themselves together for mutual benefit. The Deerfield project is ambitious and successful, so you see there a proof that coöperation and business methods can accomplish great things. A community rug business can be developed in any village or small town if the spirit of the Deerfield industries is carried out.

Two persons are most important in developing this kind of work. One is a business manager, and the other is a designer who must thoroughly understand design and colors, and who must be trained in handicrafts. The business manager attends to all the financial part of the project and places the wares before the public. The designer must plan the rugs —

shapes, patterns, and colors; she must understand the making of them, and be familiar with the problems of dyeing. The workers must coöperate in every way with both the business manager and the designer. One industry which seemed to point to success has failed because the rug-makers would not coöperate with the director; but in various localities, both in the North and in the South, rug-making has been successfully carried on by groups of workers.

The project in hooked-rug making which is being perfected at the South End House in Boston is a practical application of sane methods to develop an active craft. It demonstrates the theory of coöperation between a board of directors and crafts workers, and teaches what can be actually accomplished in an organized hand-industry, when there is a clear and definite object in view.

The South End House Industry is so much in keeping with New England in its spirit that I think a brief description of the work deserves a place in a book upon New England handmade rugs. The South End House is located in a lodging-house district in a part of Boston, to which have come men and women from Maine, New Hampshire, Vermont, and the Provinces. Here one naturally finds workers who in their youth learned from mothers and grandmothers the art of pulling in — women who are eager to find some outlet for their knowledge and their activity. One of the directors had watched the growth of the

Cranberry Island hooked-rug industry. When that was given up, she saw the possibility of carrying on a similar project at the South End House. It was the fulfillment of a dream of many years when, in the fall of 1923, the South End House Industry was actually started, to give employment to women in that district.

The workrooms at the South End House were warm and sunny. One woman told another of the industry. One by one they came to revive their knowledge of the handicraft; to carry on friendly intercourse with others — a thing which transplanted women in large cities often find so strangely lacking; to give expression to that craving for artistic expression which is the natural inheritance of all normal women; and to earn money which was to make life more comfortable for them. After a while there were about ten women, sometimes more, working at rug-making all the time.

In order to make any hand industry a success there are a number of details that must be perfected. First, there is the business side of the venture. You have your products; they should be disposed of to the best advantage of all concerned. The South End House Industry is not a money-making proposition for the directors. Its object is far superior to that. Nevertheless, the venture is naturally expected to pay its own way, so to speak, to furnish income for the crafts workers, to pay for the materials used, to take care of certain incidental and overhead expenses, and to meet the cost of placing the products before the public. The rug-makers are paid a certain price per square foot, — a sum which is fair to the women and makes the day's work satisfactory to them, — and the rugs are handled through certain arts-and-crafts shops in various large cities and resorts, as well as at the House itself.

The designer who has charge of the hooked-rug making at this South End House is a craftswoman trained in design and color, and anxious to make the rugs as nearly perfect in workmanship as is possible. All the rugs are made under her supervision, and the process is directed in detail by one of the workers who has the necessary knowledge to act as forewoman.

The stencils used for the rugs are carefully chosen and developed to make a type which the designer hopes will be so characteristic that a rug made at the South End House may be recognized at once. Only oblong rugs are made, but they are carried out in various sizes to meet the requests of purchasers. Some of the patterns are modern in conception, such as the "mille-fleurs" with its gay little clusters of varicolored flowers upon a tan background, the quaint "gull" design, proclaiming its desirability for use in the nursery or in the bathroom, and the attractive Spanish pattern which the designer has worked out to be used in houses of the South or

Southwest, where a hooked rug of typical New England style would be entirely out of place. Other patterns were evolved from antique rugs, keeping their best qualities and eliminating undesirable features. The "rope" pattern has the veritable atmosphere of rugs made in an ancient farmhouse kitchen. The "all-flower" is an adaptation of the floral design at its best, without the overelaboration of the hooked-rug patterns of the Civil War period. Neither is the popular "scroll" forgotten; it appears in some of the designs.

All materials used in the rugs are new. Even-meshed burlap makes the foundations. New cotton goods are used for the filling of the cotton rugs; new flannel is cut up for the woolen type. Cotton and wool are never mixed, you will notice. The filling material is all hand-dyed. The basement of the South End House has been turned into a laboratory, and there a young woman, who has studied the craft and who thoroughly understands the technique of dyes, experiments and gives the makers of the rugs exactly the right shades to make their products really beautiful. Big kettles of dyestuffs boil and bubble; in go pieces of undyed flannel, to come out later as glowing fabrics of rich hues.

Rugs are not the only products of the frames and hooks which the workers at the South End House use so successfully. They pull in patterns for stool tops, make trimming bands for wool dresses,

HOOKED-RUG MAKING AS A COMMUNITY INDUSTRY

and work hooked collar-and-cuff sets with fine wools and viyella flannels. An artist interested in this industry brought back the news from Paris that the centres of fashion are interested in pulled-in accessories for women's clothes, and introduced to the designer the idea of making collars for evening capes. They are very simply made, only white wool pulled through without any pattern at all, but one can picture the beauty of a white cape softened with one of these hooked collars.

So it must not be overlooked that the hooked-rug work at the South End House teaches a lesson. It proves that there is an opportunity for the development of the handicrafts of early America, a chance to do what has been accomplished by reviving distinctive handwork among the cottagers of England and of Ireland and among certain of the European peasants. Our American localities developed their own arts and crafts when it was necessary to make all things by hand. May the best of them be revived!

Now, let us talk of the selling of homemade rugs, from the point of view of the gift-shop owner or of the woman who deals in early American antiques. Perhaps you are such a woman and have an artistic shop or a quaint old house filled with antiques, tucked snugly away in one of the river valleys of Maine, New Hampshire, or Vermont — or any other part of the country, for that matter. If so, you have responded to the popular demand and are featuring handmade rugs, both antique and modern.

Hooked, braided, and woven rugs are splendid sellers, if properly presented to the public, but there are a few facts that the dealer must know, if she is to make a success of this line of wares. The most important thing of all to remember is that shoddy, ill-made rugs only cheapen the shops where they are displayed. Naturally, antique rugs are the most sought for, and bring the highest prices, but the modern rug is not to be despised commercially. The selling points to bring to the attention of a customer — in regard to hooked rugs — are the age, the fineness of texture, the originality and beauty of the design, the choice of coloring, the kind of material used in executing (woolen rugs bring higher prices than those made of cotton goods), and the symmetry of shape.

Like hooked rugs, braided rugs depend upon the material used, the choice of coloring, and the shape, for the prices which they bring. Possibly age does not play so great a part in the selling of a braided rug as it does in a hooked rug. Lovely braided rugs are now made by crafts workers. Many customers like rugs made to order to match a certain color scheme. The finer the braids used, the more valuable the rug.

Woven rugs are good sellers only when new. Designs may be displayed in the shops, and orders taken to be carried out by a weaver on her loom.

MAKING BRAIDS FOR A "THREE-AND-THREE" RUG IS A PLEASANT
OCCUPATION WHEN THE WINTER WINDS ARE BLOWING OUTSIDE

How shall handmade rugs be displayed to the best advantage? Do not pile them all together, helter-skelter, on tables, and expect your customers to sort them over. I like the method used by the owner of an overnight inn in Vermont. Her delightful rooms are furnished in old Colonial furniture, and on the floors before some of the choicest pieces are laid lovely hooked and braided rugs. These rugs are for sale and — let me whisper a secret — all of the furniture may be purchased, too. If you have only a small gift-shop, you cannot follow this plan, for the wear and tear on the rugs would be too great. But you can display a few on the walls, or lay one or two over a small table. Then, if your customer shows interest, others may be brought out for approval.

Another form of dealing in rugs is selling antique hooked rugs in one's own home. I heard very recently of a woman who carries on such a business in her apartment. She buys only the most artistic and valuable rugs which she can discover, and sells them to her friends and to interior decorators who are furnishing country homes for their clients.

Now here is one point that I wish to bring to your attention, although it is not really a part of the commercial side of rug-making. That is the value of rug-making for classes in handicrafts in the public schools, and in institutions where crafts are promoted among the patients. Hooked and braided rugs are the best kinds for schoolchildren to make, but care must be taken that the pieces attempted are not too large and too ambitious. A loom may also be installed in the art department of a school, and instruction be given in simple weaving. Adult workers can produce all kinds of handmade rugs. In one institution with which I am familiar, the art of producing hooked rugs has just been introduced. It is a little early to pass judgment upon the results, but the workers are showing enthusiastic interest.

Ten years ago, a man interested in the revival of old-time American handicrafts mournfully told me that the art of making hooked rugs was soon to be lost. Now, I am certain that he has changed his mind. For girls and women all over the country are showing a new interest in the arts and crafts of homespun days.

Thoreau says the value of a thing is determined by the amount of life that goes into it. So home rug-making will live on, as far as the craftswoman expresses herself in the products of the rug hook, the needle, and the loom.

BIBLIOGRAPHY

Books

Abnakee Rugs............................Helen R. Albee

The John Landes Pattern Book......Mary Meigs Atwater

Principles of Design................Ernest A. Batchelder

Booklets on Hooked Rugs.............Ralph W. Burnham

Collector's Luck.................Alice Van Leer Carrick

The Next-to-Nothing House.......Alice Van Leer Carrick

Practical Book of American Arts and Crafts

Eberlein and McClure

A Book of Hand-Woven Coverlets......Eliza Calvert Hall

The Craft of Hand-Made Rugs............Amy Mali Hicks

Batiks and How to Make Them..............Peter Mijer

Dyes and Dyeing.....................Charles E. Pellew

Hooked Rugs and How to Make Them..Anna Laise Phillips

Modern Home Dyeing..............Martha Jane Phillips

Weaving and Other Pleasant Occupations

R. K. and M. I. R. Polkinghorne

New England Bygones.................Ellen H. Rollins

Magazine Articles and Service Sheets

"Service Sheets on Rug-Making"

Woman's Home Companion — Good Housekeeping — Modern Priscilla

"Everybody Is Braiding Mats"....Mary Foster Bainbridge

Ladies' Home Journal, October 1922

"Weave Your Own Rugs from Rags"....Elizabeth Boswell

Delineator, May 1926

"More about Hooked Rugs".........Leonard F. Burbank

Antiques, November 1922

"Hooked Rugs"....................Mary Johnson Carey

Antiquarian, May 1925

"Scrap Bag Rugs"..............ALICE VAN LEER CARRICK
Ladies' Home Journal, October 1921

"The Repair of Hooked Rugs"...........ANNE R. CONGDON
Antiques, August 1922

"A Memory of Grandmother's Mats"...GERTRUDE DeWAGER
Antiques, June 1925

"Have You Made One?"....................SARA HADLEY
Country Gentleman, September 1925

"Where Cottage Craft Is Plied".......ELIZABETH E. MORSE
Modern Priscilla, February 1923

"When the Clock Reel Ticked"...........AMY V. RICHARDS
Modern Priscilla, Tercentenary Number, December 1920

"Humor in Hooked Rugs"..............MABEL S. S. STONE
House Beautiful, November 1925